d States, in order to form a more perfect Union, establish justice,
the general Welfare, and secure the Blessings of Liberty to ourselves
ed States of America.

Congress of the United States, which shall consist of a Senate and House

s chosen, every second Year by the People of the several States, and the Electors
Branch of the State Legislature.
he Age of twenty five Years, and been seven Years a Citizen of the United States,
l be chosen.
States which may be included within this Union, according to their respective
ns, including those bound to Service for a Term of Years, and excluding Indians
made within three Years after the first Meeting of the Congress of the United States,
by Law direct. The Number of Representatives shall not exceed one for every
until such enumeration shall be made, the State of New Hampshire shall be
Plantations one, Connecticut five, New York six, New Jersey four, Pennsylvania
h Carolina five, and Georgia three.
cutive Authority thereof shall issue Writs of Election to fill such Vacancies.
s; and shall have the sole Power of Impeachment.
s from each State, chosen by the Legislature thereof, for six Years; and each

Election, they shall be divided as equally as may be into three Classes. The Seats

WE THE PEOPLE

The Declaration of Independence, *painted by John Trumbull. Courtesy of The Yale University Art Gallery.*

We the People

A PORTRAIT
OF THE
LIFE AND TIMES
OF THE
REVOLUTION

BY ROBERT ALDACE WOOD

HALLMARK CROWN EDITIONS

Designed by William Hunt.
Editorial Direction by Tina Hacker.
Illustrations on pages 9, 33, 53, 60 and 89
by Rich Rudish and Art Carlson.
Staff Photographers for this book:
Ronald Brown, Richard Fanolio and Masataka Miyao.
Title Lettering designed by Norval Arbogast.
Production Art by Judi Howen.

Set in Janson, a typeface designed by Nicholas Kis in 1690.
Printed on Hallmark Crown Royale Book paper.

©1975, Hallmark Cards, Inc.,
Kansas City, Missouri. All Rights Reserved.
Printed in the United States of America.
Library of Congress Catalog Card Number: 74-17863.
Standard Book Number: 87529-405-7.

WE THE PEOPLE

Chapter I

ON THE EVE OF THE REVOLUTION

Always, it seems, there is something crisp, invigorating and rejuvenating about the cool, clean air of autumn. Did the men who gathered in Philadelphia in the September of 1774 taste liberty on the wind or see, along with the incipient change in seasons, a turning point for their own land? As the bell in old Christ Church summoned them to destiny, did they guess that they would never again be Englishmen?

Here for the first time men from varying religious and cultural backgrounds, representatives of colonies so diverse and distinct that their very words sounded in accents strange and foreign, measured each other across the stately expanse of Carpenter's Hall. Here Edward Rutledge of South Carolina met fiery-eyed John Jay of New York. Rhode Island's Stephen Hopkins, gnarled and old like the New England apple tree, clasped the hand of Virginia's lordly Peyton Randolph.

But John Adams was there, too, sizing up these men for whom history held something glorious. He finds them a true cross section of the colonies — some with youth, some with age, some hotheaded and some temperate:

September 1, 1774, Thursday. *In the evening, all the gentlemen of the Congress who were arrived in town met at Smith's, the new city tavern, and spent the evening together. Twenty-five members were come....Mr. William Livingston, from the Jerseys, lately of New York, was there. He is a plain man, tall, black, wears his hair; nothing elegant or genteel about him. They say he is no public speaker, but very sensible and learned, and a ready writer. Mr. Rutledge, the elder, was there, but his appearance is not very promising. There is no keenness in his eye, no depth in his countenance; nothing of the profound, sagacious, brilliant or sparkling in his first appearance....*

Carpenter's Hall (interior), Philadelphia, where the First Continental Congress assembled.

Independence Hall, Philadelphia.

John Jay

Peyton Randolph

John Adams

John Witherspoon

All the portraits on this page, courtesy of The Independence National Historical Park Collection.

2. Friday. *Dined at Mr. Thomas Mifflin's, with Mr. Lynch, Mr. Middleton and the two Rutledges with their ladies. After coffee we went to the tavern, where we were introduced to Peyton Randolph, Esquire, Speaker of Virginia, Colonel Harrison, Richard Henry Lee, Esquire, and Colonel Bland. Randolph is a large, well-looking man; Lee is a tall, spare man; Bland is a learned, bookish man.*

These gentlemen from Virginia appear to be the most spirited and consistent of any. Harrison said he would have come on foot rather than not come. Bland said he would have gone, upon this occasion, if it had been to Jericho.

3. Saturday. *Breakfasted at Dr. Shippen's; Dr. Witherspoon was there. Col. R. H. Lee lodges there; he is a masterly man. This Mr. Lee is a brother of the sheriff of London, and of Dr. Arthur Lee, and of Mrs. Shippen; they are all sensible and deep thinkers. Lee is for making the repeal of every revenue law, the Boston Port Bill, the bill for altering the Massachusetts Constitution, and the Quebec Bill, and the removal of all the troops, the end of the Congress, and an abstinence from all dutied articles, the means — rum, molasses, sugar, tea, wine, fruits, etc....He would not allow Lord North to have great abilities; he had seen no symptoms of them, his whole administration had been blunder. He said the opposition had been so feeble and incompetent hitherto that it was time to make vigorous exertions.*

Mrs. Shippen is a religious and a reasoning lady. She said she had often thought that the people of Boston could not have behaved through their trials with so much prudence and firmness at the same time, if they had not been influenced by a superior power....Dr. Witherspoon enters with great spirit into the American cause. He seems as hearty a friend as any of the natives, an animated Son of Liberty. This forenoon, Mr. Caesar Rodney of the lower counties on Delaware River, two Mr. Tilghmans from Maryland were introduced to us... and we drank sentiments till eleven o'clock. Caesar Rodney is the oddest-looking man in the world; he is tall, thin and slender as a reed, pale; his face is not bigger than a large apple, yet there is...spirit, wit and humor in his countenance.

Talk of the Times

As evident in this selection from John Adams's diary, this was a momentous occasion — men drawn together on the eve of revolution by the felt necessities of the times. But it was not unique. From Boston to Charleston, other colonists talked about the schism between mother country and colony. And a taproom as far away as the New Hampshire grants may have been witness to the following scene:

Through the big door of the Catamount Tavern came Remember Channing. And a strange sight he was, too, for a clergyman. One gray stocking was rumpled and slightly askew. His face was broken out in a warm sweat, and he fanned himself with his cocked hat so that the animal odor of his greased wig blew through the room and mixed with the pungence of ale, cider and the tang of smoky cedar burning away to drive out the flies.

"How-come-ye-so, Reverend?" sang out Soames Baker.

"Why, by way of the Cruikshank's, the Stebbins's place, the Boynton's and the widow Rutledge's," laughed the minister. He was greeted with an answering peal of laughter from the group resting around an old trencherboard.

"And what news of Mrs. Rutledge?"

"Oh, she is in a very sorry way, I fear. Caught a pleuritical disorder from removing her clogs before entering church last Sunday."

"And what did you prescribe?"

"Why, a hot toss pot of good flip and punch, naturally."

"Seems like you're one to take your own medicine, Doctor."

The colonies responded to the passing of the Boston Port Bill with this broadside, printed in June, 1774. Courtesy of The Massachusetts Historical Society.

"The good Lord wanted it that way, else He would not have written, 'Give strong drink unto those that be of heavy heart.'"

"Why, that's so, and there's no denying the force of scripture."

"And what news have you friend Baker, to keep you and these other worthies chattering over your blackjack tankards?"

"Bad news, I fear, Reverend." Baker pulled nervously at the ribbons in his knee breeches. "I hear that rump Congress in Philadelphia has passed the hateful Suffolk Resolves entertained by those turncoats and footpads of Boston."

"Rump Congress! How can you say that when we've sent our own good John Sullivan there! And as for the Suffolk Resolves, no man who is not lost to all honor can wonder that free men should condemn the odious Coercive Acts. Men born to be free Englishmen have every right by nature and nature's God to form a government of their own, to levy their own taxes, to gather arms and form their own militia."

"Aye, Reverend, I was born to be an *Englishman*, and it makes me mad to think such harpies and brigands as we have now in Philadelphia would conspire to scuttle the Galloway Plan — a plan that every right-thinking man loved for proposing union with Britain. Those blockheads obliterated any mention of the Galloway Plan from their minutes. Why? To keep it from the people. I say the Suffolk Resolves they passed instead are no more than words on a privy wall."

Baker ended by sullenly fingering his buttons made of gold piasters and drinking deep of his mug of ale.

"And what say you, Aunt Barrow, and you, Jack Whittaker?" The reverend turned to a woman done up in striped ticking closed with hooks and eyes (not real buttons), and the man beside her in brown tunic, buckskin breeches and honest round-toed shoes. In spite of the generous cedar smoke, he wore leggings to frustrate the deprivations of the flies and mosquitoes.

"Well, now," Whittaker answered, "I have always been one hearty in the cause of liberty. It's a good country this is. My connections down in Marblehead, for instance, have fourbled and fivebled their fortunes in precious little more than two years. But if they can't trade 'cept in British ports, and if the colonial ports close, and what with taxes on every little thing, they'll be reduced to burning lard just to warm their hands. I say God save us all, for futurity is decidedly unfathomable!"

Destruction of Tea, Boston Harbor, Dec. 16, 1773, *painted by Darius Cobb in 1902. Courtesy of The Ancient and Honorable Artillery Company of Boston.*

The Green Dragon Tavern, Boston, where tradition says plans were laid for the Boston Tea Party. Courtesy of The American Antiquarian Society.

To be sure, for most colonists on the eve of war, futurity was decidedly unfathomable. But the coming revolution — a rebirth of ideas as well as a civil war — was hardly of a sudden making. It was talked and argued and *advocated*, to use a newly coined term of the day, in the Green Dragon, the Bunch of Grapes, the Catamount, in all the taverns and taprooms of the day.

Indeed, it was at the local public houses, not the village green, that the flames of revolution were kindled. In 1774 at the Queen's Head Tavern, the Sons of Liberty and the Vigilance Committee met to protest the landing of the British tea and to lay plans for dumping it. As John Adams remarked apropos of the trade in molasses and rum, "I know not why we would blush to confess that molasses was an essential ingredient in American independence."

The Local Brews

Especially in New England, the tavern was a community institution like the meetinghouse, school or local mill. Of these, it stood preeminent. Tavern keepers were often selectmen or deacons of the church. Women were welcome in the tavern, as was our Mistress Barrow, a relation addressed in the custom of the day by her last name as *Aunt Barrow*.

The infamous tax stamp, imposed by the British government in 1765, was a major cause of dissent in the colonies. Courtesy of The Massachusetts Historical Society.

The "blackjack" tankard was made of leather and coated with wax to make it ale-worthy. Courtesy of Colonial Williamsburg.

In Virginia, the free flow of ardent spirits played an important role in three of young George Washington's political victories. In Maryland and the middle states, a special local beverage was brewed, according to this old rhyme:

For planters' cellars, you must know,
Seldom with good October (ale) flow,
But Perry Quince and Apple Juice
Spout from the tap like any sluice.

And in Pennsylvania, one man in six made the formidable Monongahela rye whiskey. In 1791 the frontier counties of Fayette, Allegheny, Westmoreland and Washington foreshadowed the sooty skyline of modern-day Pittsburgh as fragrant smoke drifted upwards from the chimneys of no less than 5000 log stillhouses.

People were reared from childhood on the phantasmagoria of potent brews. In old Albany, for instance, records show that "pastors and people... vied in the production of the best cherry, and raspberry, and strawberry brandy." These fruity potions took the place of vitamins in the minds of Albany mothers who prescribed doses to cure children of worms and bellyaches.

Whiskey slaked the thirst in summer, warmed one's toes in winter. It sanctified the contract of marriage and soothed mourners at burial services. New England towns were obliged by law to supply liquor for pauper funerals because proper respect for the dead required tippling as well as coffin burial.

Ever-present whiskey was available at the county clerk's office when the trial list was made up. Jurors, soldiers and sailors all expected their daily dram. A minister making pastoral rounds might come home pretty "how-come-ye-so" because each household was supposed to offer him a drink. A new journeyman owed his shopmates a round "to pay his footing." A new coat called for "a sponging." Liquor, a way of life, loosened the tongue and entered into the language in a variety of forms.

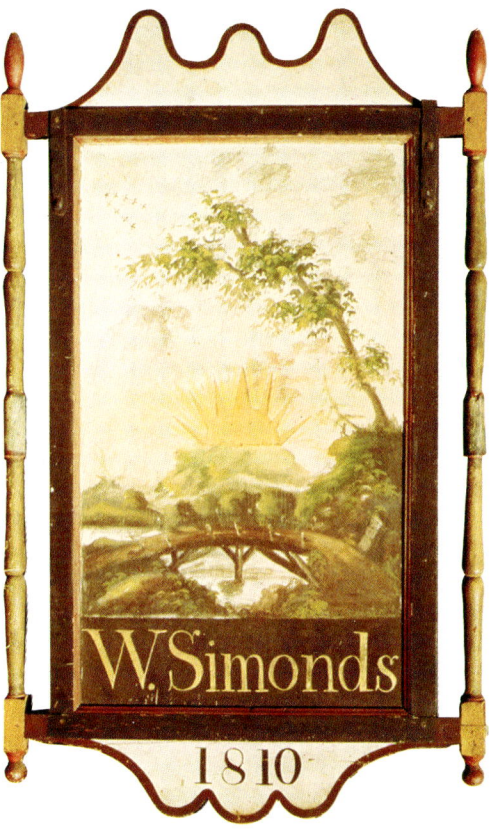

The proprietor's name was often the most prominent feature of tavern signs in the colonial period. Courtesy of The Lexington Historical Society.

Interior of the Buckman Tavern in Lexington, Massachusetts. This house, built in the early eighteenth century, was used as a tavern between 1740 and 1815.

*Noah Webster
Courtesy of The Independence
National Historical Park Collection.*

Americanisms — A Linguistic Revolution

Indeed, it was our language, so different from the mother tongue that Englishmen recommended dictionaries of "Americanisms," that best exemplified our new "American" revolutionary attitudes. Noah Webster issued a linguistic declaration of independence when he wrote:

Several circumstances render a future separation of the American tongue from English necessary and unavoidable....Numerous local causes such as a new country, new associations and some intercourse with tribes wholly unknown in Europe will introduce new words into the American tongue. These causes will produce, in a course of time, a language in North America as different from the future language of England as the modern Dutch, Danish and Swedish....We have therefore the fairest opportunity of establishing a national language and of giving it uniformity and perspicuity in North America that ever presented itself to mankind.

The plain people, those like the ones gathered in our Catamount Tavern, stoutly gave their hearts and their devilish inventive tongues to Webster's scheme for emancipating the American language. The period from the gathering of the Revolution to the turn of the century was one of immense activity in the concoction and launching of new Americanisms; more words and phrases of native invention came into the language then, than at any time between the landing at Plymouth and the 1848 discovery of gold in California.

Born into a verbal culture where "forensic disputations" raged in meeting, church and tavern; where every colonial college stressed rhetoric in its curriculum; nurtured in a land where the very conditions of life favored curiosity over convention, American iconoclasts and innovators forged a new language struck full of odd epithets like "blockheads, brigands and footpads," and stirred to quixotic verbs like "fourbled and fivebled," and lastly, added spice with implausible adjectives like "imkeeled" and "homicidious." Their inventive language paralleled their experiments in politics.

Great Britain stood aghast at this "barbarous English." Yet it was the democratic spirit which framed the words that drew the old world's greatest censure. Scandalized, the *Edinburgh Review* found that Americans made it "a point of conscience to have no aristocratical distinctions—even in their vocabulary." They think "one word as good as another, provided its meaning be as clear."

Oftentimes the press would single out a lone rebel linguist to pillory. Among Thomas Jefferson's signal achievements was the invention of the verb "belittle."

According to the *European Magazine and London Review*, it was an upstart indiscretion every bit as repugnant as his Declaration of Independence.

Belittle [it roared]! What an expression! It may be an elegant one in Virginia, and even perfectly intelligible; but for our part, all we can do is to guess at its meaning. For shame, Mr. Jefferson! Why, after trampling upon the honor of our country and representing it as little better than a land of barbarism — why, we say, perpetually trample also upon the very grammar of our language....Freely, good sir, will we forgive all your attacks, impotent as they are illiberal, upon our national character; but for the future — O spare, we beseech you, our mother tongue!

Soon English reviews began belaboring and "belittling" everything on this side of the Atlantic. This, of course, just raised the feisty and stubborn national conceit of Americans. And as the Revolution drew to a close, there was a widespread tendency to reject English precedent and authority altogether.

At the end of the war, certain members of Congress proposed that the use of English be formally prohibited in the United States and Greek substituted. One authority, C. A. Bristed, reports that the change was rejected on the grounds that "it would be more convenient for us to keep the language as it is, and make the English speak Greek."

Clearly, in life and language, the taverns and taprooms saw as much that was revolutionary as did any battlefield. Indeed, in so many ways, the men and women of these United States would never again be *English*.

This engraving, published in 1775, shows American discontent with British rule in the colonies. Represented are (1) King George, (2) a Frenchman, (3) a Roman Catholic priest, (4) the House of Commons, (5 and 6) two American yeomen, (7) Brittania blindfolded, (8) Quebec and (9) Boston in flames. Courtesy of The Massachusetts Historical Society.

Chapter II

THE INFANT CITIES

Colonial doorways in Elfreth's Alley.

New York — Boston — Philadelphia: these were the considerable metropolitan nerve centers in revolutionary America. Already they exerted the intoxicating, siren lure of the big city. Countless Pollyannas and earnest country bumpkins were drawn to them. In 1749, stagestruck Nancy George ran away to New York to become a star! Yes, the rags-to-riches lure of the city is fully two hundred years old.

To young Americans then, these yeasty forerunners of the twentieth-century megalopolis represented all there was in their world of reason and culture, sin and wantonness. Absolutely true. Diaries of the day give us a fascinating picture of cities where art and riot flourished side by side and incredibility was the normal state of things.

These cities were alive with the edgy, animated energy of people consciously pulling themselves up by the bootstraps. Peddlers hawked in the streets till their tonsils ached. Carriages and hacks rumbled through mud wallow streets or creaked through small fogs of dust. Packs of dogs and scavenging hogs routed about with eddies of street people till "the rattle-gab" proved so distracting to Boston's John Adams that "to put the mind into a stirring, thoughtful mood" he would flee to the serenity of the family farm in Braintree.

The eighteenth-century mercantile passion bred a competitive cosmopolitan air. Cakes and beers were dispensed in ornate, gingerbread gazebos in the Battery of New York. In Philadelphia, oyster vendors solicited the fashionable theatre crowds. And in dark, vermin-ridden recesses of the city, kidnappers, pickpockets and cutthroats, willing to kill for the price your hair would bring at the wigmaker's, coughed and spit and drank and waited.

Elfreth's Alley in Philadelphia, a street lined with beautifully preserved prerevolutionary houses, looks today very much as it did two hundred years ago.

A map of Boston as it appeared in 1769. Courtesy of The Massachusetts Historical Society.

Yankee Fashions

Colonists looked to the city as a life-style pacesetter. New York, Boston and Philadelphia were centers of fashion and extravagant dress. One look down a city street revealed a cosmopolitan mix of people whose rank on the social ladder was easily visible in a frock coat with pretentious buttons made of Spanish dollars, or in homely round-toed shoes and shiny leather breeches.

Here and there one might see a dandy in a long-tailed coat and red-heeled shoes, or an aristocrat in a heavy silk waistcoat with satin embroidery, knee breeches, white stockings and buckle shoes.

Working men wore heavy linen shirts, breeches of striped ticking, a leather apron and a heavy coat of duroy or a buckskin tunic called a "wamus," open down the front and secured by belts or ties…never by upperclass buttons.

While gentlemen wore the famous cocked hat of the period, laborers sweated under slouch hats: beaver in winter, straw in summer. In typically practical Yankee fashion, their boots and shoes were made to fit either foot. Breeches were full with no opening flap. When pants wore shiny on the seat, they were simply turned around and worn shiny side front.

The Revolution began to bring an end to dandified

ornamentation in clothing. Colors were dark but never dull. Warm browns, dark orange, blue, purple and so-called french green became popular. Jewelry was no longer worn.

General Baron von Riedesel, commander of German forces aiding the English, had occasion to see many homespun patriots, and he sniffed at their taste in fashion:

One can see in these men here assembled exactly the national character of the inhabitants of New England. They are distinguished from the rest by their manner of dress. Thus, they all, under a thick, round, yellow wig, bear the honorable physiognomy of a magistrate. Their dress is after the old English fashion. Over this they wear, winter and summer, a blue blouse with sleeves, which is fastened round the body by a strap. One hardly ever sees any of them without a whip. They are generally thickset, and middling tall; and it is difficult to distinguish one from another.

The ways of speech and dress are as significant for identifying the cast of mind of the ordinary person as are papers and manifestos for the lettered and learned. Just as Americans embraced in their language the democratic and unorthodox doctrine that one word was as good as another, so in their dress they began to discard tailored distinctions in class. In short, it became "difficult to distinguish one from another."

George Washington, the man who thought it was sufficient to be addressed as "Mr. President" rather than as "Highness" or "Excellency," also thought it fitting and proper to appear at his inauguration accoutered in a simple, dark brown broadcloth suit—the first cloth manufactured in the United States at Worcester, Massachusetts.

Fashion was a burning and divisive issue in young America, with overtones that reflected Tory and patriot philosophies. George Washington had strong views on the matter of appropriate dress. He once advised his nephew:

Decency and cleanliness will always be the first object in the dress of a judicious and sensible man; a conformity to the prevailing fashion in a certain degree is necessary; but it does not from thence follow that a man should always get a new Coat, or other clothes, upon every trifling change in the mode, when perhaps he has two or three very good ones by him. A person who is anxious to be a leader of the fashion, or one of the first to follow it will certainly appear in the eyes of judicious men, to have nothing better than a frequent change of dress to recommend him to notice....

In the city, colonial *belle dames* frequently went about in wooden clogs with leather straps and poplar soles. These individual "boardwalks" were necessary for walking on cobblestones—where there was cobbled pavement—and mud where there wasn't. They were about as noisy as horseshoes, however, and ladies were requested to remove them before entering church.

At home, a colonial matron would wear everyday black leather shoes and for special occasions—dress slippers of colored kid, morocco leather, or velvet, satin, brocade, or damask—all richly embroidered.

Quilted petticoats made of layers of dainty, colored silk and satin were very popular. They were worn under the *watteau sacque*, a loose gown of dimity or chintz, named for the French designer Antoine Watteau. The skirt was long, but was looped up to show the petticoats.

Captain Samuel Chandler *and* Mrs. Samuel Chandler, *painted by Winthrop Chandler in about 1780. These portraits show the typical fashions worn by colonials of the upper middle class. Courtesy of The National Gallery of Art, Washington, D.C. Gift of Edgar William and Bernice Chrysler Garbisch.*

Both men and women of means fancied wigs, for which a person's head was shaved and measured. And from 1760 onward, ladies' hairstyles began to rise. Hair was pomaded with grease so that the decorative white powder would stick. Wool, bran, horsehair and cushions on wire foundations were employed to build the hairdo up to three feet or more. The top was often adorned with flowers and feathers or surmounted by a cap or bonnet called a *calash*.

After her hair was fixed, a woman would sleep sitting up to keep from mussing it. The hairdo lasted as long as three weeks, and so did the discomfort. Mice, lice and other vermin so infested these pompadours that special head scratchers were provided to ease the itching. Designers created long, jewel-encrusted head scratchers to dignify this fundamentally unsanitary fashion.

It is interesting to note that whereas Washington preached temperate haberdashery at his nephew, he frequently gave in to the whims of his niece, Nellie. She was reportedly the first woman in America ever to wear a bridal veil.

Even a Frenchman, Marquis de Chastellux, was taken aback by "the rage for dress among patriot women." He wrote:

The rage for dress among the women in America, in the very height of the miseries of war, was beyond all bounds; nor was it confined to the great towns, it prevailed equally on the seacoasts, and in the woods and solitudes of the vast extent of country, from Florida to New Hampshire. In traveling into the interior parts of Virginia I spent a delicious day at an inn, at the ferry of Shenandoah, or the Catacton Mountains, with the most enchanting, accomplished and voluptuous girls, the daughters of the landlord, a native of Boston, transplanted thither; who, with all the gifts of nature, possessed the art of dress not unworthy of Parisian milliners, and went regularly three times a week to the distance of seven miles, to attend the lessons of one de Grace, a French dancing-master, who was making a fortune in the country. In one of my journeys, too, I met with a young Frenchman, who was traveling on the business of the celebrated M. de Beaumarchais, and was uncommonly successful in his amours, of which I speak from personal knowledge. On my inquiring the secret of his success, he assured me, and put it beyond a doubt, that his passe-partout, *or master key, consisted in a fashionable assortment of ribands, and other small articles contained in a little box, from which, in difficult cases he opened an irresistible and never failing battery.*

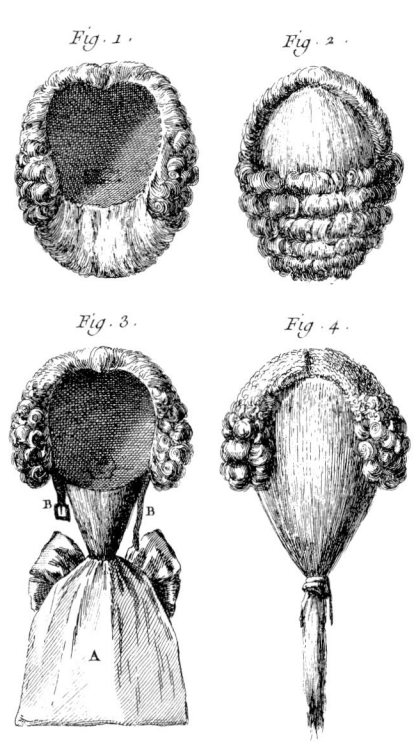

Wigs commonly worn in the eighteenth century, as pictured in Diderot's Encyclopedia. *Figures 1 and 2 show "bonnet wigs" or "short wigs," and figures 3 and 4 show "bag wigs," named for the black taffeta bag that held the long hair at the back. Courtesy of The Bettmann Archive.*

The Colonial Woman

In other respects, American women found life, even in the city, hard and earnest due to the demands of childbearing. Gottlieb Mittelberger, one of an unceasing stream of curiosity seekers from the Old World, wrote of Philadelphia: "Whenever one meets a woman, she is either pregnant, or carries a child in her arms, or leads one by the hand."

But to be truthful, colonial women defied generalization. They were neither fashion plates nor queen bees. They proved a testy lot, durable as rawhide, serving with their tough-minded, tabasco-tongued men in a violent and primitive land. Mobs were not uncommon in the city, and like as not they were mobs of women. Some stripped and tarred offensive members of the community. The women of Schoharie County, New York, for instance, made manifest their indignation at being served eviction notice by the local sheriff by dragging him through the street, riding him on a rail and sending him home with two broken ribs and one remaining eye.

The same spirit, directed toward worthy ends, made for remarkable testimonials to the business acumen and accomplishments of colonial women. Eliza Pinckney, daughter of a British army officer, founded the multimillion dollar indigo dye industry of South Carolina. Mrs. Martha Smith carried on in her husband's stead as the master of a testy, leathernecked lot of Long Island whalers. Likewise, the irrepressible Mrs. Sueton Grant of Newport, Rhode Island, became a merchant princess in command of a sizeable fleet of ships left to her by her husband. The very liberated Mrs. Grant was a tough and determined adversary. She believed in standing up for her rights in court—literally. Once, convinced that her counsel was bungling her law case, she rose to press the fight herself, secured her verdict and probably became the first woman to practice law in any English-speaking country.

Colonial women were by no means barred from commercial pursuits. Opportunities were as varied as imagination, and America's women did not lack for imagination. They did anything that came to mind. In New York, for instance, widows were accustomed to opening saloons; and New York State looked upon the grant of a tavern license to a widow as a modest form of social security. In nearby Bordentown, New Jersey, the redoubtable

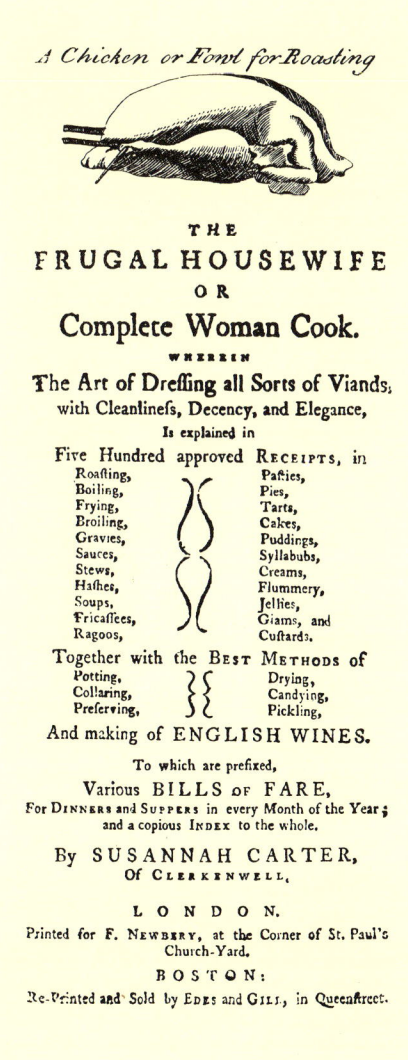

Title page for The Frugal Housewife, *a cookbook printed in Boston in 1772. Courtesy of The American Antiquarian Society.*

Twelve-year-old Ann Mead, like so many little girls her age, stitched samplers to demonstrate her domestic skills. This sampler is dated 1773. Courtesy of The Philadelphia Society for the Preservation of Landmarks.

Patience Lovell Wright, widowed with three small children, turned to her long-standing hobby of molding effigies in clay and wax and, indeed, she prospered at this unique endeavor. By 1771, Mrs. Wright had an extremely successful New York showing à la Madame Tussaud.

America was already a nation of individuals. While some families taught their daughters the niceties of etiquette and the simple pleasures of needle wisdom, others — even families of quality — raised young ladies who smoked pipes, drank in an age of ferocious drinkers, and swore in a time when an oath was an oath and a curse could get you kicked out of town.

And colonial girls blanched not at the banal carnalities of the flesh. Neither did their menfolk. Possibly because the well-worn gossip about scandals among European nobility excited emulation, John Hancock maintained a mistress until the advanced age of thirty-nine, when he married Dorothy Quincy. Robert Hunter Morris, chief justice of New Jersey and governor of Pennsylvania, never married at all, but fathered three children, one of whom followed in his father's footsteps as chief justice.

The Reverend Samuel Locke, president of Harvard, lost his job in 1773 for getting his housekeeper with child. In Philadelphia, the Presbyterian synod found a pastor guilty of fornication, though a month later it allowed him to resume his duties because of "signs of true repentance."

No less a man than Aaron Burr, onetime vice-president of the United States and grandson of the great Protestant divine, Jonathan Edwards, was sued for divorce on the grounds of infidelity…at the age of 78.

In Pursuit of Pleasure

Then as now, American cities were thought to be the centers of unbridled philandering. To a large extent this was true. Boston had a large and well-equipped bon ton district. The riverbank half cellars of Philadelphia became brothels. By the 1770s, New York had at least five hundred prostitutes — nearly two percent of the population.

But philandering was a frame of mind in a feisty new world. Well-bred William Byrd II of Virginia took his bad habits pretty casually, for he often remarked in his diary: "Said my prayers…committed uncleanness with her, for which God forgive me."

This formal garden, located in Philadelphia's Independence National Historical Park, is representative of those found in the eighteenth century.

Elaborate colonial kitchens, such as this one at Mount Vernon, Virginia, were often built by well-to-do families. They were a separate structure from the house and were located near the garden.

Benjamin Latrobe sketched this friendly game of billiards at a country tavern. Courtesy of The Maryland Historical Society.

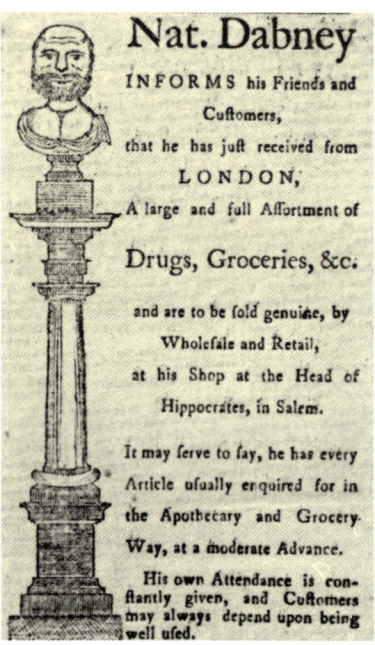

Illustrated advertisements such as this were very rare in eighteenth-century newspapers. Courtesy of The American Antiquarian Society.

When not wenching or drinking, colonial city slickers were apt to be gambling or shooting pool. "The Game of Billiards is not less in Esteem for Its Variety and Amusement, than for the fine Exercise it occasions," wrote John Drew, author of *Treatise on the Game of Billiards, 1771.* "At the same time," he continued, "the Powers necessary for this Game are so gentle, that it is equally adapted to the Entertainment of the Fair Sex; and many Ladies now play the Game to a very great Degree of Nicety and Perfection."

Perhaps so, and yet it is difficult to imagine an eighteenth-century Willie Mosconi, handicapped as he would have been with tipless pool cues resembling hockey sticks. Nevertheless, billiards was a good excuse for drinking and socializing. Pool parlors and amusement pavilions like the Spring Garden and Center House were thriving in Philadelphia. Citizens of Richmond, Virginia, played at the Swan Tavern on Tenth and Broad, and at Eagle Tavern on Main and Twelfth streets.

These amusement parlors were wicked, sinful places. At least, so said the reform elements of the colonial city. According to Salem's William Bently, there was trouble in River City. In 1793, he twice wrote in anguished protest of his distress over the "young persons" who "indulged in Billiard tables in the public houses." It was feared that young persons would learn to gamble there. And in 1788, the city fathers of New York passed a law subjecting tavern keepers to fine and imprisonment should they allow cock fighting, gaming, card playing, dice, billiards...or shuffleboard in their establishments. Drunkenness was punishable by three shillings or two hours in the stocks.

On both counts reformers failed. Cities sustained and enhanced their long-standing reputation as little Babylons. One New England town was embarrassed when its blacklist of town drunks grew so long that visitors mistook it for the list of eligible voters.

Neither were reformers successful in stamping out gambling. Bets could still be made on the street in front of taverns, and many colonists wagered away all but their wives and families.

Washington's army was decimated by the ravages of "pitch and toss," an innocent game of chance on which his men would squander their time and gamble away their arms and munitions. The great majority of the country was subject to what we might now call "Las Vegas fever," symptomatic of a worldwide philosophy of competition, mercantilism and the boundless possibilities of acquisition.

Boston, however, displayed a raffish Yankee ingenuity in tapping the zest for gambling. Starting in 1762, several lotteries were sponsored for the refurbishing of Faneuil Hall. These lotteries consisted of several thousand tickets which sold for two dollars each.

Gambling was also newsworthy — attracting crowds, tavern business and mention in the local tabloid. In 1786, the *New York Gazette* reported the incident of a man who "for a trifling wager, et fifty boiled eggs, shell and all. He performed the task in about fifteen minutes being elevated on a butcher block during the operation."

For those not suitably edified by the performance of an egg glutton, taverns turned moralistic and strove to secure a more uplifting, horizon-widening kind of entertainment. Some contemporary advertising read as follows:

Aorson's Tavern —"The Only Lecture of the Season...by a man more than thirty years an Atheist!"

A Faneuil Hall lottery ticket bearing the famous John Hancock signature. Courtesy of The Bostonian Society.

The Merchant's Coffee House—Dr. King, lately from South America, has arrived from Charleston with a collection of Natural Curiosities...a Male and Female of the surprising species of the Ourang Outang or the man of the Woods...the Sloth, which from its sluggish disposition will grow poor from traveling from one tree to another...the Baboon, of different species and a Most Singular Nature...Monkey, Porcupine, Ant-Bear, Crocodile, Lizard, and Sword Fish, Snakes of various kinds and Very Extraordinary; Tame Tiger and Buffalo. 10 A.M. — 10 P.M.

The taproom of the New England and Jersey Hotel—The Learned Pig....Every Evening!...his sagacity too well known to need a vain, puffing, elusive advertisement...the proprietor will state only what the Pig Actually Performs!...Reads! Spells! Tells the time of day, the date, day of the month! Distinguishes color! Tells how many people are present!...and to the astonishment of many of the spectators will Add, Subtract, Multiply and Divide...also will Divine Cards, besides a variety of entertaining matters of Politics, Love, and Matrimony!

Drama and Melodrama

Where the blandishments of the Learned Pig palled, jaded city dwellers could always go to the theatre. Although mid-century Massachusetts looked upon stage plays as agencies of the devil and strictly forbade their performance, canny troupers invented the ploy of billing their productions as morality plays. In Newport, Rhode Island, in 1761, the stage company found it necessary to advertise *Othello* as "Moral Dialogues in Five Parts, Depicting the evil effects of jealousy...and proving that happiness can only spring from the pursuit of virtue."

Massachusetts was somewhat backward in this respect. Elsewhere, audiences enjoyed the standard repertoire of Shakespeare, Otway, Powe and Cibber. Just as Yankee

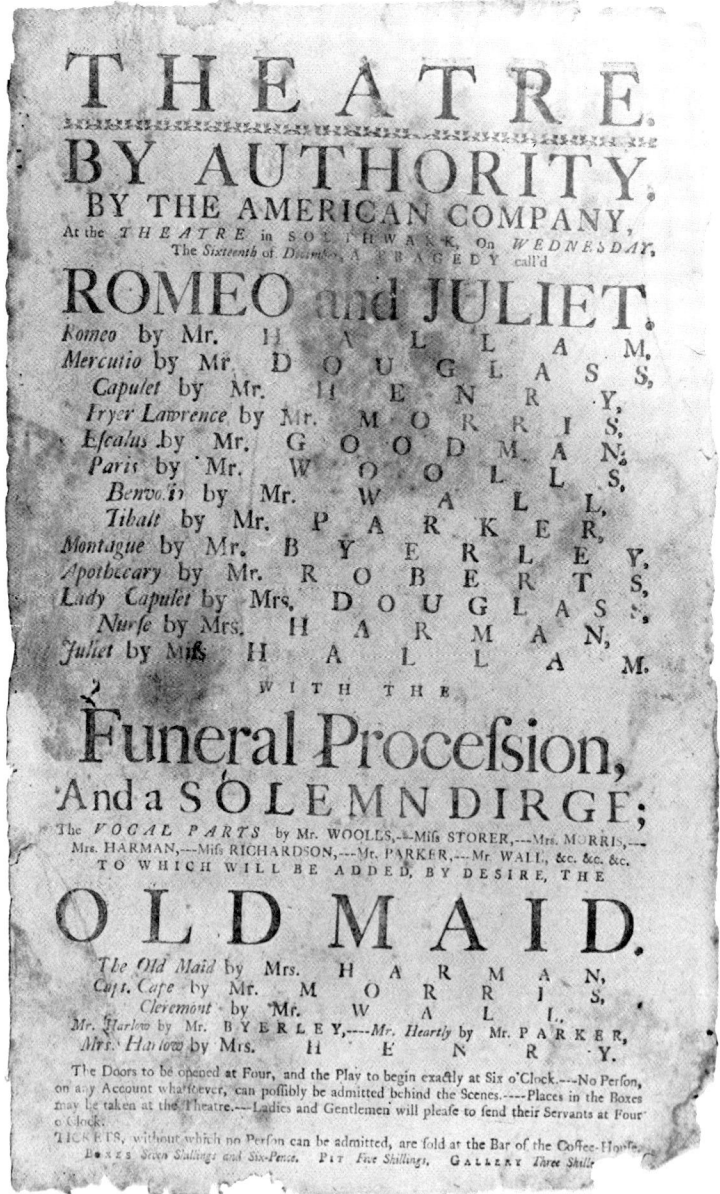

A rare theatrical broadside advertising a double bill of Romeo and Juliet *and* The Old Maid. *Courtesy of The Library Company, Philadelphia.*

businessmen had cajoled their clergy into selling evil lottery tickets for some worthy cause, so in the matter of theatrics they proved that the silver standard was stronger than the golden rule. Suspicion of moral turpitude on the stage was quickly routed by editorial salvos like this from the *New York Postboy*—"Actors promote the Circulation of Cash by employing Masons, Carpenters, Taylors, Painters, etc., and generally leave their money where they got it!"

With the British occupation of major American cities came new impetus for the theatre. General John Burgoyne himself dashed off a farce called *The Blockade of Boston*. His was an unforgettable opening night, as described in H. E. Sudder's 1876 edition of *Men and Manners in America One Hundred Years Ago*:

The curtain was about to be drawn for the farce, when the actors behind the scenes heard an exaggerated report of a raid made upon Charlestown by a small party of Americans. One of the actors, dressed for his part, that of a Yankee sergeant, came forward upon the stage, called silence, and informed the audience that the alarm guns had been fired, and a battle was going on in Charlestown. The audience, taking this for the first scene in the new farce, applauded obstreperously, being determined to get all the fun there was to be had out of the piece, when the order was suddenly given in dead earnest for the officers to return to their posts. The audience at this was thrown into dire confusion, the officers jumping over the orchestra, breaking the fiddles on the way, the actors rushing about to get rid of their paint and disguises, the ladies alternately fainting and screaming, and the play brought to great grief.

Theatre did much to advance the intellectual accomplishment of young America. People read plays as literature. The libretto of the most recent stage play was bought as eagerly as the latest novel. If a company wished to produce a play for which they lacked the libretto, they could be reasonably sure of borrowing it from someone in town. One such libretto-less company advertised in 1751, "If any gentleman or lady has the farce called *The Intriguing Chamber Maid* and will lend it awhile to the players, it will be thankfully acknowledged."

This advertisement shows that bookdealers in colonial times often printed and bound their volumes as well as sold them. Courtesy of The American Antiquarian Society.

Arts and Letters

This was just one aspect of the yeasty and vigorous intellectual life growing up in the cities. Although learned men like Dr. David Ramsey were apt to sniff at the feeble state of American arts and letters—"there is so little intercourse in a literary way between the states"—there is evidence that America read much. *Scot's Magazine* reported a bookfair held in New York that sold 520,000 volumes. Henry Lemoine found all bookstores in New York, Philadelphia and Boston doing a brisk trade. The Fellows of the American Society of Language met to polish the native tongue, to "correct, enrich and refine it," until that happy day when "perfection stops their progress and ends their labors."

This unusual design decorated a scarf and is decidedly Loyalist in viewpoint, as evidenced by the inscription around the outside border. Courtesy of The Germantown Historical Society, Philadelphia.

Conscientious men and women organized to distribute Bibles and redeem the "lower orders" from pauperism and illiteracy. Even backwoodsmen aspired to philosophical undertakings. Ethan Allen hoped to write a liturgical opus that would free the world from the stultifying myths of Christianity and substitute for them a "system of Natural Religion" based on "scientific observation and the strictest logical reasonings."

In an age when rationalism held sway, Dr. Benjamin Franklin was revered for his landmark strides in natural science. But he was not alone. James Logan, secretary to William Penn, had experimented with the hybridization of corn. George Washington, an agribusinessman at heart, strove constantly to build up his soil and even practiced tree grafting. He was the first man in America to cultivate alfalfa, and contemporaries indicate if once wound up, he could talk your ear off, preaching about the problems of the Hessian fly.

The Loyalist Viewpoint

One of the great calamities that burdened the young republic was the fact that many of its brightest minds were Loyalists. The dispersion of talent to England and Canada after the war brought immeasurable hardship to the country.

During the war, however, America's cities were centers for refugee Tories, and no account of the infant cities would be complete without some mention of the Loyalist viewpoint.

In Philadelphia, many Quakers remained loyal to the king. Boston and New York, while under British control, succored many Tory families. Often, these Loyalists were remnants of a toppled colonial aristocracy whose brocades and silks were tattered and thin now, whose pride was mainly pretense.

New York's taverns frequently hosted Tory entertainments, singing of Loyalist songs and feasting. But naturally there was bitter, bewildered conversation, too. Loyalists chafed at the lackluster war waged by the British army. They wondered at the cruelty of the patriots and the abrupt reversal of fortunes that had swept away the old order in favor of upstart shopkeepers. Still, they were apt to put on a brave face at Loyalist gatherings, where conversation might have sounded like the one that follows:

Benjamin Franklin
Courtesy of The Independence
National Historical Park Collection.

"My, such a levee! Even Sam Faunces never planned a party more elegant and agreeable."

"Why, Mrs. Lemaire, how can it help but be the most pleasant party possible when we have the best people from all New England here? Doctors, officials, Anglican clergymen and members of the bar. There's Dr. James Lloyd, Dr. Thomas Bolton, some of the Chandler clan from near Worcester, Massachusetts, some Sewalls and Fitches — most of the first families of the colony, all the more distinguished in exile."

"What wouldn't those Sons of Liberty do for an invitation here?"

"Those Sons of Violence be damned. Do you know that they've mobbed men of the cloth — churchmen — godly, pious gentlemen like Henry Caner of King's Chapel? The mobs cry, 'Down with the church, the Rags of Popery!'"

"Aye, John Bristol, you and Mrs. Lemaire talk of the mobs, but *I've* seen them. Worse than wolves. A wolf kills quickly. These street dogs — bloody wretches who grew up out of the pissmire in the streets — they seized upon a Boston tradesman, one Malcolm. They were but boys, many of them. They picked a fight with the old man. He was stripped naked in the winter cold and afterward tarred and feathered. They dragged him off in a cart like ants with a piece of carrion, beating him with clubs, whipping him and making sport of the pitiful creature. They left him at his door. My God, what a sight for the man's wife and children. When they took the gobs of tar off, they say the flesh came with it!"

"Curse the traitors! I wish I were a man so that I might fight back."

"Yet, Mrs. Lemaire, there are a score of Loyalist regiments now. There are thousands more men ready to die on the side of justice as against anarchy. But the British, Mrs. Lemaire, the British will have nothing to do with us! My gorge rises when I think of it."

"Well, I'll say this. There's one Englishman who has plenty to do with one Mrs. Joshua Loring."

"You mean General Howe! Fie, in nine months in Boston, Eliza Loring was Howe's only conquest — a regular bedroom soldier he."

"If you ask me, gentlemen, the British Antony has sacrificed an empire for the sake of his Boston Cleopatra!"

"I wonder that her husband stands it!"

"Hasn't he got what he wants? The British have given him a fat position as

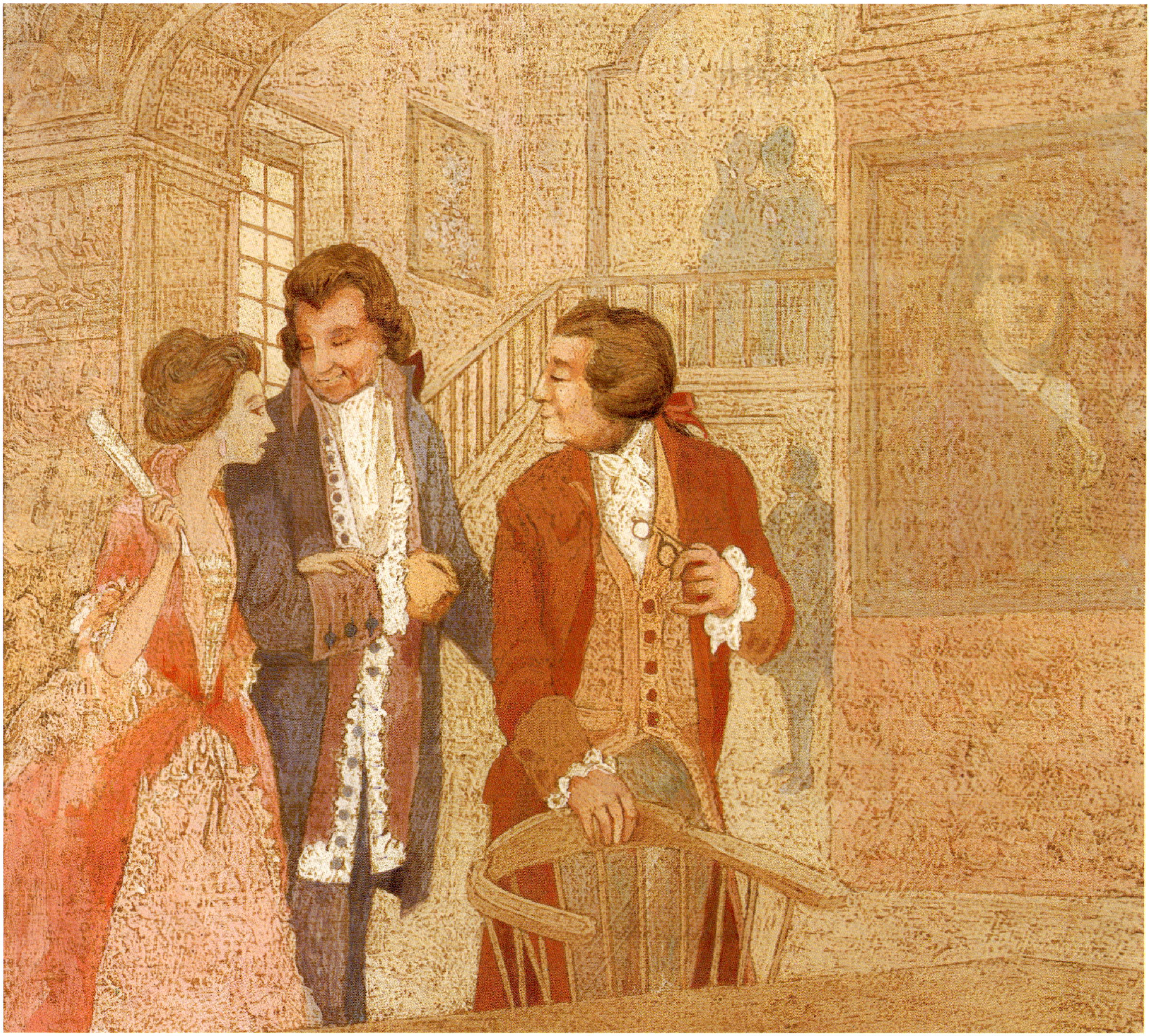

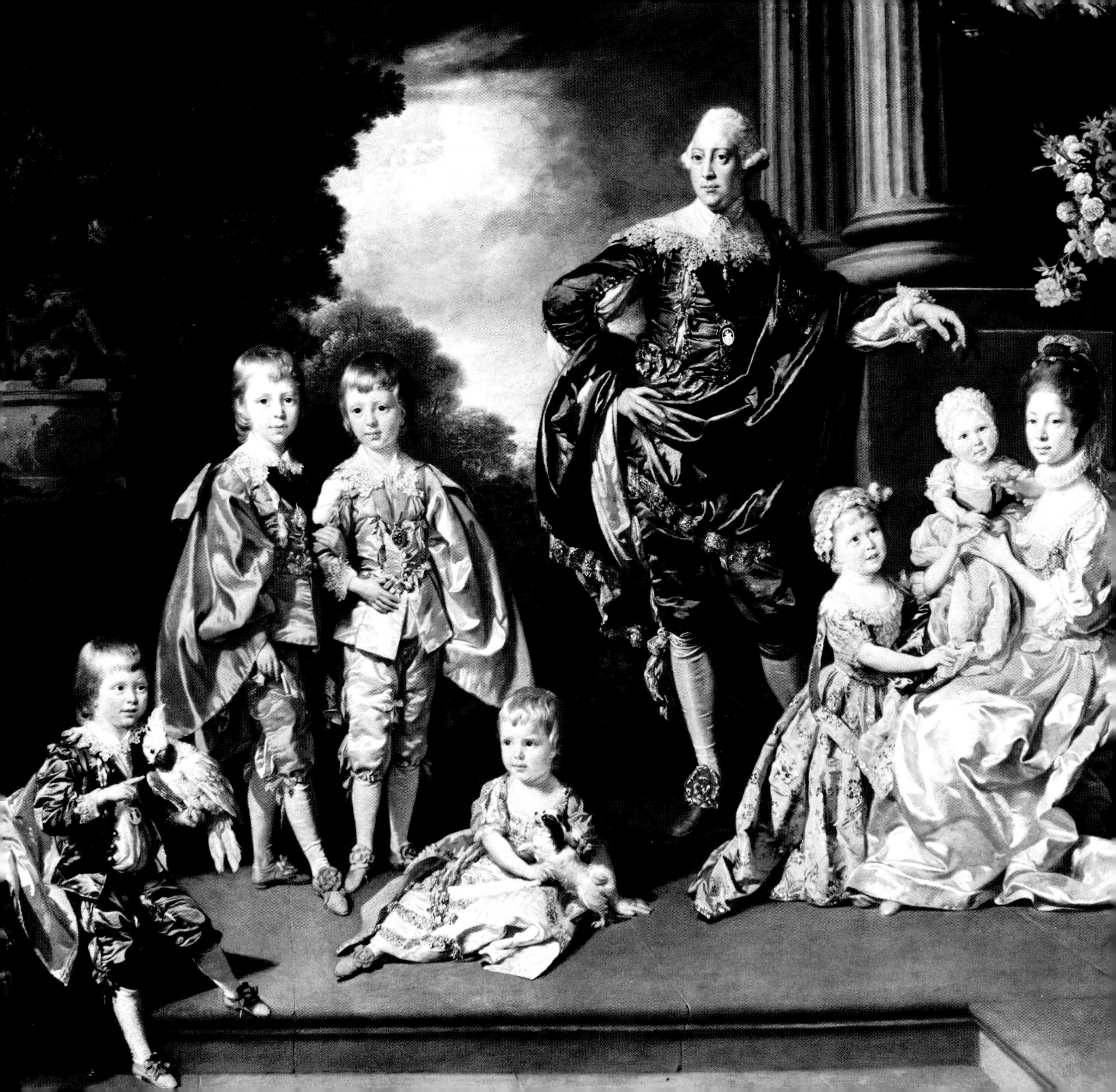

commissary to the army. But come, let's show the ladies the newest steps, and there's cold pastry and porter waiting besides."

"Now, that's fare for a God-fearing man!"

"Aye, have you heard that that great infidel Jefferson eats *ice creams* and something he calls *macaroni!*"

"No wonder the man's a rebel, with a stomach like that."

"They're all alike, that rebel breed. Sam Adams is a damned demagogue. Washington is a debtor. And Hancock, that pitiful dunderhead who finished at the bottom of his class at Harvard, is a bloody smuggler and swindler with a price on his head!"

"The Devil take them all!"

Many thoughtful men in the colonies embraced the Loyalist view. To them, the revolutionists and their patriot committees were little better than mobs, threatening the liberty of loyal subjects and tyrannizing decent folk. Although few Americans felt the oppression of King George — the specter which demagogues like Sam Adams and Tom Paine constantly conjured up — many had seen the wanton destruction of rebel mobs. Ironically, freedom of the press, freedom of speech and assembly — the same liberties that would be guaranteed by the Bill of Rights — were often flaunted by the revolutionists. Search and seizure was common, with dirty, wolfish patriots pawing through the petticoats and personal possessions of helpless Loyalist families.

It was easy for British sympathizers to believe that all rebels were alike, to link the camp followers and criminal opportunists with high-minded men of ideals like Washington and Jefferson.

Unfortunately, to be branded a Tory or Loyalist amounted to excommunication. Many Loyalists ardently worked for relief from misguided British colonial policies, but they brooked no armed rebellion. In effect, they wished to work for change through the system, the establishment extant at the time. But rebel leaders demanded a passionate commitment; it was often a case of those who are not with us are against us. They made life hard for neutrals and temperate Loyalists, and as a result, America lost many able men at a time when she most needed them. The concentration of Tories added some sophistication to the squalor of the cities, and they would be sorely missed.

King George III and Family, *painted by John Zoffany in 1771.*
Courtesy of Her Majesty Queen Elizabeth II, Copyright Reserved.

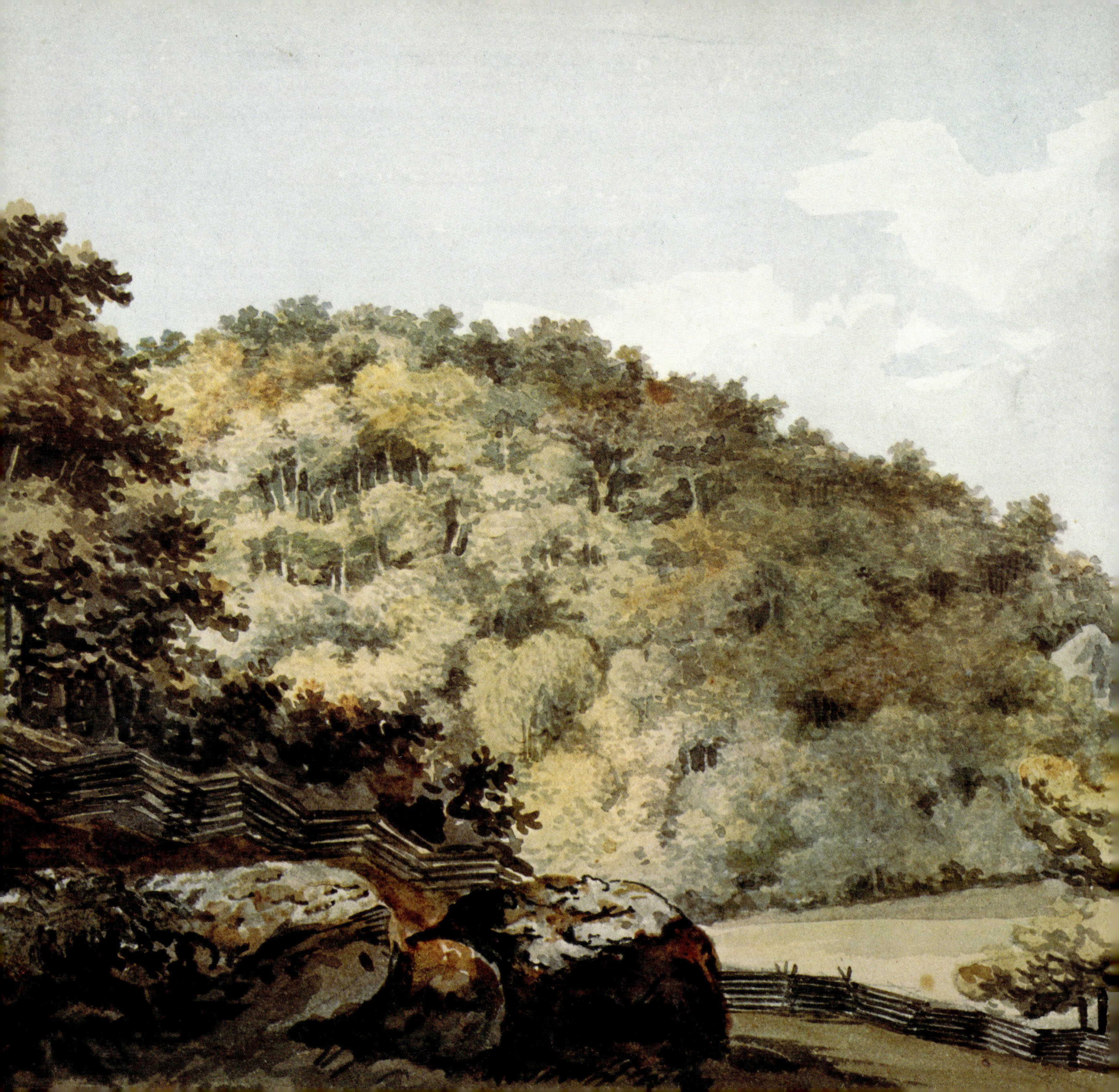

Chapter III

AT HOME IN RURAL AMERICA

America on the eve of revolution was a rich and undisturbed land whose virgin vistas called out to men with fruitful promise. This was a country of big sky, undefiled waters and boundless opportunity. So trackless was America west of the cities that years might pass before two men glimpsed the same wooded glen or valley.

Forests in that era were rich with northern elms and birches and long-standing oaks. They bore a totally different character than the woods of today, heavily planted with the omnipresent pine. Then a man might shoot his own game, although neither schooled in stealth nor expert marksmanship. Why, canvasback ducks, busily gorging themselves on wild celery, gathered thick along the banks of the Susquehanna and Potomac rivers! Men talked matter-of-factly of shoals of perch so plentiful in Tiber Creek that a fisherman could gather a fine mess by firing a shotgun into them.

Pheasant, partridge, pigeon, turkey, squirrel, rabbit, crab and oysters came regularly to colonial tables. Deer, however, had been wantonly slaughtered by burning great stretches of forest, and by 1800, venison would be considered a delicacy.

Far-flung communities checkered the wilderness. Breaking out of the burly woods with busy and businesslike exuberance, they greeted travellers with a sudden flash of color, the scent of fresh-broke sod, ripening hay and the song of flails at work in the fields.

A generation removed from the Revolution, Pennsylvania chronicler George Lippard describes Germantown, one such typical village in the year 1777:

The roofs of the ancient village, extending in one unbroken line along the great northern road, arose gray and massive in the sunlight, as each corniced gable and substantial chimney looked forth from the shelter of the surrounding trees. There was an air of quaint and rustic beauty about this village. Its plan was plain and simple,

View of the James River, Virginia.

Waterfall and quarry.

The illustrations which are reproduced at left, above and on the following two pages were painted by Benjamin Latrobe. This author-illustrator-architect travelled widely throughout the colonies in the late eighteenth century and recorded his impressions through charming watercolors such as these. Courtesy of The Virginia State Library.

Benjamin Latrobe's impression (above) of Yorktown, Virginia, and (right) his painting of a fishing expedition on the Appomattox River in Cumberland County, Virginia. Courtesy of The Virginia State Library.

burdened with no intricate crossings of streets, no labyrinthine pathways, no complicated arrangement of houses. The fabrics of the village were all situated on the line of the great northern road, reaching from the fifth milestone to the eighth, while a line of smaller villages extended this "Indian file of houses" to the tenth milestone from the city.

The houses were all stamped with marks of the German origin of their tenants. The high, sloping roof, the walls of dark gray stone, the porch before the door, and the garden in the rear, blooming with all the freshness of careful culture, marked the tenements of the village, while the heavy gable-ends and the massive cornices of every roof gave every house an appearance of rustic antiquity.

Around the village, on either side, spread fertile farms, each cultivated like a garden, varied by orchards heavy with golden fruit, fields burdened with the massive shocks of corn, or whitened with the ripe buckwheat, or embrowned by the up-turning plow!

Inside the houses of Germantown, comforts were sparse. Many walls wore only a homely coat of plaster. Joists and crossbeams showed in every ceiling, scoured white and planed smooth. Wallpaper and painting were rare save in the homes of the moderately well-to-do. General Neville's Pennsylvania home, for instance, was remarkable because it was furnished with such marvels as carpets, mirrors, pictures and prints, and an eight-day clock.

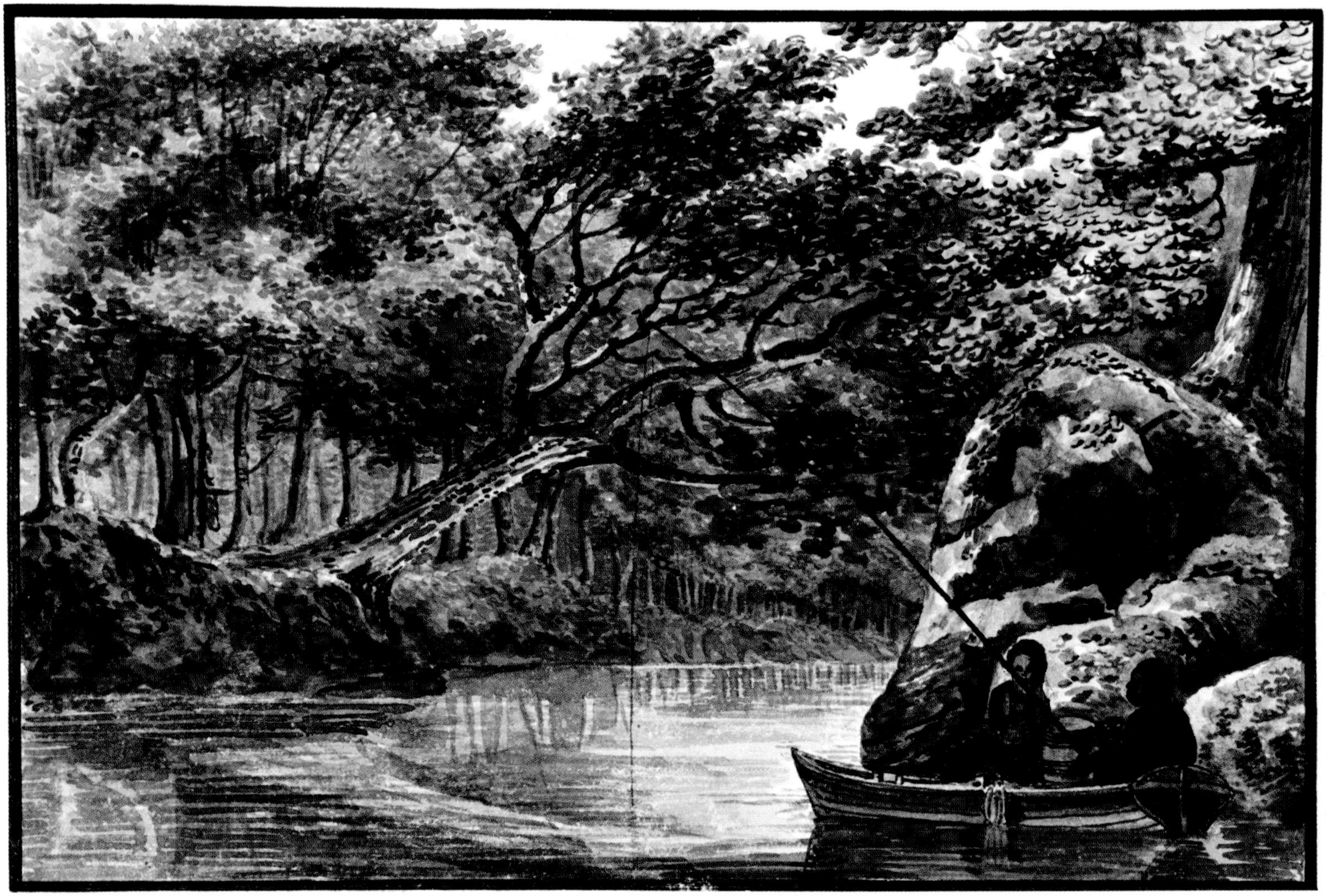

A reproduction (right) of an eighteenth-century bedroom. Courtesy of The Concord Antiquarian Society. A Chippendale clock (below) made in Philadelphia in the late eighteenth century by Thomas Lindsay. Courtesy of The Germantown Historical Society.

Furniture was built for utility. Contrary to current fashion, almost everything sat well off the floor on stout legs. Chippendale sideboards, bureaus, bedsteads, cabinets and dressing cases were set a foot high in tidy fashion.

Metal gutters projected from almost every home to the center of the street. Much to the distress of passersby, this battery of gutters resembled Niagara Falls in rainy weather.

Cellars and garrets hung redolent with dried herbs. Bins of apples, potatoes, turnips, beets and parsnips were marshaled in swelling rows. There were hogsheads of corned beef, barrels of salt pork, tubs of hams being salted in brine, tunnekins of salt shad and mackerel, firkins of butter, kegs of pigs' feet, tubs of souse, kilderkins of lard. Stout racks bulged with barrels of cider, vinegar, and sometimes beer, rum and a pipe of Madeira. On a long swing shelf sat tumblers of spiced fruit, and "rolliches," headcheese and strings of sausages — all German delicacies that recall Benjamin Franklin's remark, "I saw few die of hunger; of eating, one hundred thousand."

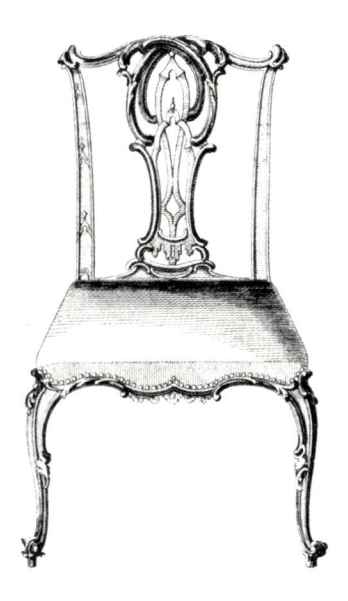

An etching (top) of a Chippendale chair. Courtesy of The Virginia State Library. A teapot (above) imported from China in 1785 bearing a very popular early patriotic design utilizing the new "American" eagle. Courtesy of The Valley Forge Historical Society. The entrance hall (at left) of the Grumblethorpe house in Germantown, through which the doorway to the rear garden can be seen. Courtesy of The Philadelphia Society for the Preservation of Landmarks.

Travel and Tribulation

A visitor from the northernmost American settlements, like Maine, where the fundamental comfort of glass windows was unknown until 1745, might well envy his relatives and connections to the south. But there was little pressure to keep up with the Joneses, if only because the Joneses — or Delanceys, Stuyvesants and Carters — were so remote. To reach the burgeoning cellars and groaning boards of Pennsylvania, or to plunge even deeper into the tidewater and plantation country of Maryland and Virginia, a man had to traverse a wilderness.

The hardships of inland travel reached a point of downright peril. Roads were interrupted by large streams, rivers and tidal waters. Travellers, carriages and skittish horses were crowded aboard flimsy ferries to be poled or rowed across, often by dirty, destitute Indians suspected of "homicidious" inclinations.

Rivers that are crossed on spans of steel today were formerly roiling death-traps. Even so redoubtable a hero as General Horatio Gates found his courage waver when he saw how shaken were the incoming passengers from their ferry across the Hudson.

Of the rivers crossed in travelling by the common road from New York to Philadelphia, the Hackensack and the Passaic had ferries, the Raritan only a ford. According to Morse's *American Geography of 1789*, three floating bridges made of logs fastened together had been thrown across the Schuylkill River in Pennsylvania.

Sign (above) used for over a hundred years at a gate of the Columbia Turnpike Co., between Great Barrington and Hudson, New York. Courtesy of The Library of Congress. View of the Newburg Bridge (below) which spanned the Merrimack River in Massachusetts; etched in 1793. Courtesy of The American Antiquarian Society.

Read between the lines, and this advertisement in the *Cincinnati Centinel* will convince you of the hardships of river travel in ferry, barge and broadhorn.

Two boats will travel, between Cincinnati and Pittsburgh. The first boat leaves Cincinnati at 8 o'clock, and returns to Cincinnati so as to sail again in four weeks. The proprietor of these boats having naturally considered the many inconveniences and dangers incident to the common method heretofore adopted of navigating the Ohio, and being influenced by the love of philanthropy, and desirous of being serviceable to the public, has taken great pains to render the accommodations on board as agreeable and convenient as they can profitably be made. No danger need be apprehended from the enemy (Indians), as every person on board will be under cover, made proof against rifle or musket ball; convenient port-holes for firing will be found on each boat.

Ever sensible to turning hardship to advantage, early American entrepreneurs established river insurance companies at three points along this route: Cincinnati, Pittsburgh and Limestone.

Overland travel was no better. A traveller often found himself lost, mapless in a welter of roads that wound, for the sake of economy in labor and expense, over pine ridges. To make matters worse, early engineers would often build highways with a drainage ditch in the middle, rather than sloping the road toward the left and right shoulders, as is the custom today. This center drainage system often resulted in more swamp than road, notwithstanding which, John Mercereau carried passengers between Elizabethtown and Trenton, New Jersey, in the remarkable time of a day and a half in a stage vehicle aptly, if prematurely, named "The Flying Machine."

Benjamin Latrobe, a visitor in young America who stayed on to partly design and build the Capitol building in Washington, suffered the manifold exasperations of early American travel. Fellow tourists can sympathize with Latrobe, who received directions just as confusing as today's "you can't get there from here" variety. He notes in his journal:

Col. Skipwith's Cumberland County.

To get my person to this place has been the work of much labor and contrivance.... The road indeed was straight enough. I rode without fear till I fancied I must have exceeded the seven miles of distance I had to travel. I then turned into a plantation, the third opening only which I had met with in these eternal woods. A...man came to the gate, who in a long speech bewailed my having missed the proper turning to the right in this infallibly straight road. It was about four miles behind me. The day

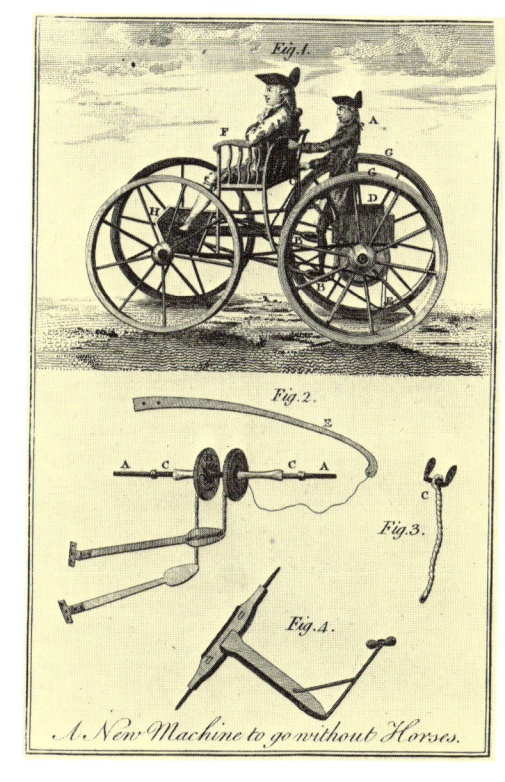

A design for a very early "horseless carriage," published in 1774. The power was provided by the poor fellow on the right. Courtesy of The Library of Congress.

was excessively sultry, and my horse appeared as tired as his rider. Nothing, however, could be done but to go back, and I got nearly the following directions:

"I am right sorry, master, you are so far out in this hot day. It is very bad indeed, master. You must, if you please, turn right around to your right hand, which was your left, you see, when you were coming here, master. I say you turn right around to your right hand, which was your left hand, and then you go on and go on about two miles or two miles and a half, master. It's very bad indeed to have to ride so far back again on so hot a day, and your horse tired and all; but when you have got back again about two miles or two miles and a half you will see a plantation, and that plantation is Dicky Hoe's. That's on your right hand now as you're going back, but it was on your left hand when you were coming here, you see, master. The plantation is Dicky Hoe's on your right hand, right handy to the road, and there is a house with two brick chimneys on it; but it is not one house, it only looks like one house with two brick chimneys,...but it is really two houses; you will see it right handy to the road a little way off, with two brick chimneys, on your right hand, which was your left hand when you were coming here...."

"Now I know all about it," cried I, fatigued. "Good morning, my good fellow, and thank you many times." I rode off in a full trot, and when he was out of sight he was still calling out to me about my right hand which was my left.

Marriage and Family Life

Wherever a man travelled across the length and breadth of this nation-to-be, he met with certain tendencies and attitudes of mind which would in time be perceived as national traits. Among these was faith in the concept of family. Franklin, that font of pithy wisdoms, called families the "sacred cement of all societies."

The Copley Family, *painted by John Singleton Copley.*
This picture depicts family life in the eighteenth century
with fine detail, accuracy and much tenderness.
Courtesy of The National Gallery of Art, Washington, D.C.

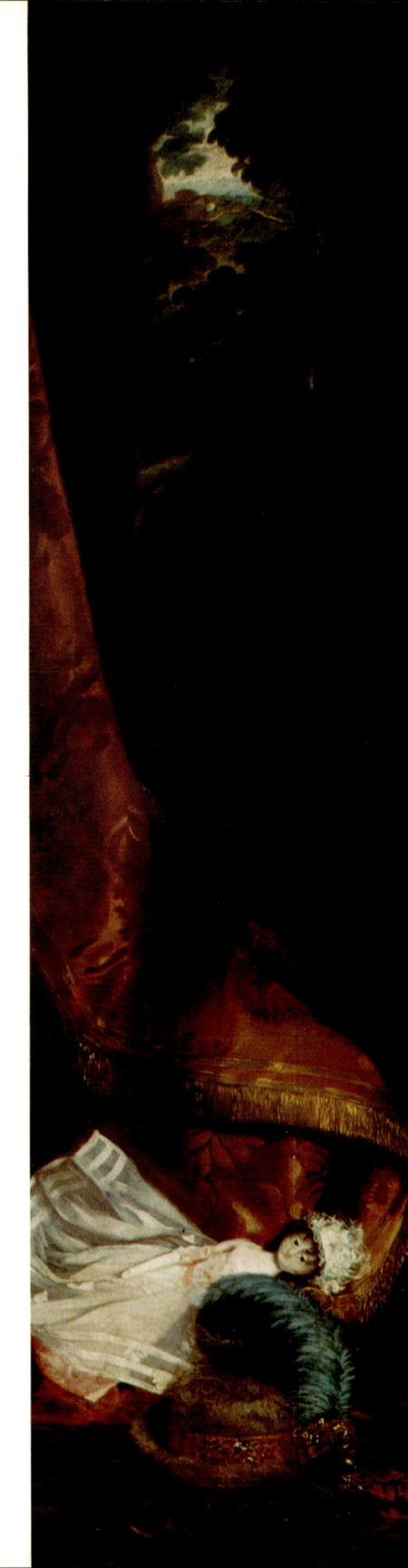

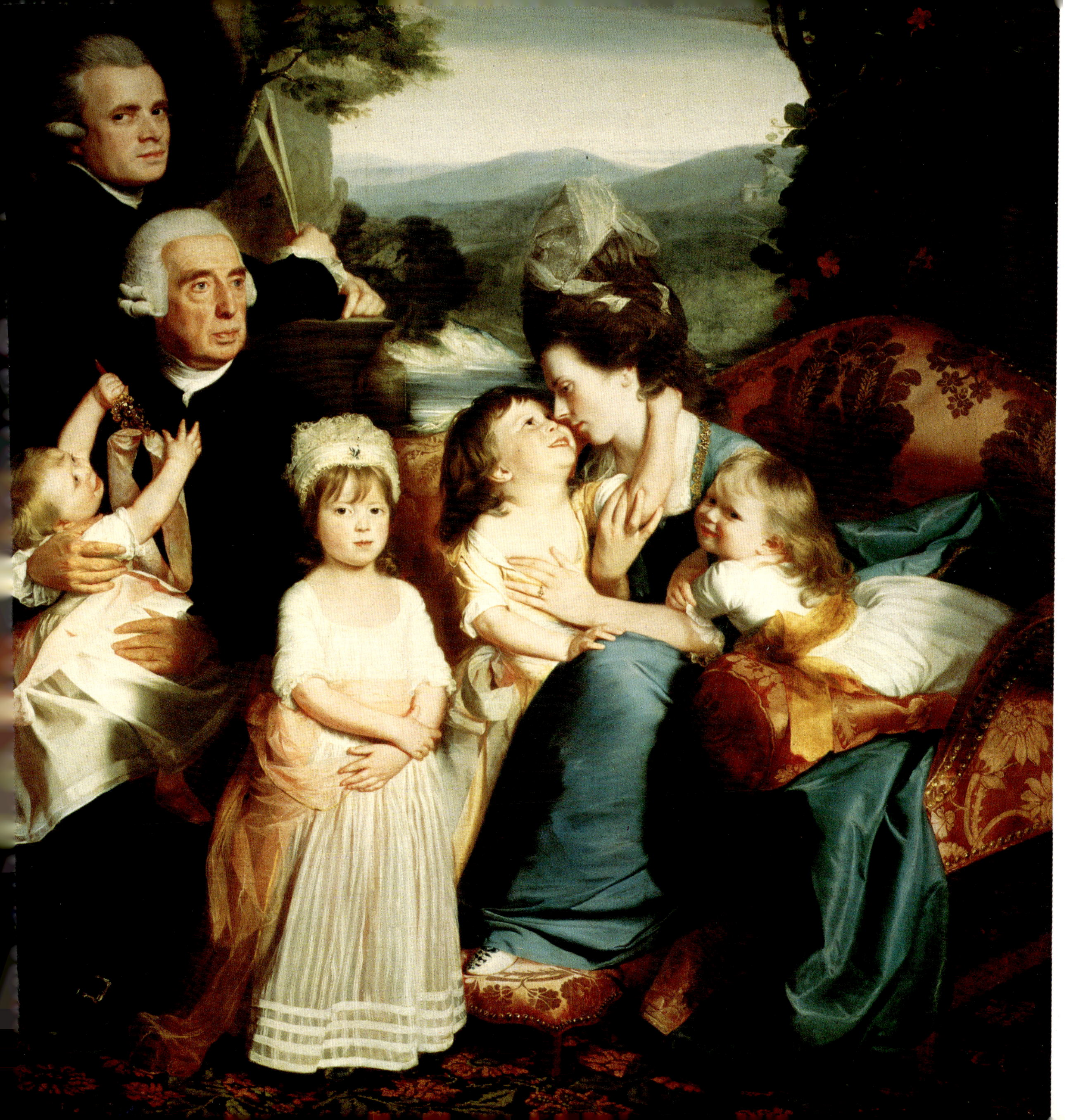

Here in America, the family was an economic necessity sanctioned by religious custom and secular law. Wallflowers and bashful bachelors were suffered not at all.

Handsome land grants were provided newlyweds in certain New England communities. Marriage had its rewards and celibacy its drawbacks. At one time, matchmaking legislators in Maryland and Pennsylvania actually taxed bachelorhood. By law, a single man was forbidden to dwell alone in Connecticut. He was simply assigned quarters wherever and with whomever the town fathers wished. Confirmed bachelors were thoroughly reviled. "The odd half of a pair of scissors!" snorted Dr. Franklin.

Contrariwise, society nodded somewhat approvingly at the good providers. Fertility in Mrs. Sarah Thayer was lauded in a sobering inscription on her tombstone: "She'd fourteen children with her at the table of the Lord."

Just as abrupt as our country's passage from colony to nation was the transition of native Americans from children to adults. There was virtually no period of adolescence in early America. The basic assumption was that children were miniature adults, and they were treated accordingly. Twelve-year-old boys occasionally wore wigs, and their sisters suffered under enormous hair arrangements. One passed all too quickly from a world of marbles, leap frog and blindman's buff to a world heavy with family responsibilities. Boys reached majority at sixteen, at which time they became taxpayers and members of the militia. At the same age, many girls were already wives and mothers.

Young love was natural and not to be denied. Sarah Rutledge, the mother of the South Carolina patriot John Rutledge, married, for example, at fourteen; Ursula, daughter of the prominent Virginia planter William Byrd I, at sixteen. The Benjamin Latrobes, however, like most parents, had reason to doubt the wisdom of their offspring. Their oldest girl, Lydia, stunned them by falling in love at the age of thirteen with Nicholas Roosevelt of New York and New Jersey, a great-great-uncle of Teddy Roosevelt. At 37, Roosevelt was less than four years younger than his prospective father-in-law. After four years of secret meetings, and a "year's cooling off period" to no avail, Lydia eventually married with her parents' blessing.

Courtship in the Colonies

Courtship in the colonies was a curious blend of business and pleasure. For many, marriage was a legal contract, holy vow and social milestone. Romance entered into it hardly at all.

In recounting Walter Franklin's courtship of Hannah Bowne, Anne Wharton tells us that the suitor confronted Hannah's father and "they talked of matters that each thought would interest the other, Franklin not forgetting to praise the cows he had seen in the barnyard, but no mention was made of the maid who milked them." After two more such visits, with no more dalliance than permitted in an "ardent glance," Franklin ended his anemic courtship and married the girl.

Others, happily, proved more amorous, for the rather romantic tradition of the "kissing bridge" took hold in several areas. At such a bridge, a favorite trysting place, a young man might steal a kiss — in fact, custom demanded it!

Elsewhere, principally in the New England states, sweethearts took to "bundling." During the cold northern nights, boys and girls were permitted to conduct their wooing snuggled under the bedcovers, provided they were circumspect and fully clothed. This arrangement offered lovers a degree of privacy otherwise hard to find in the cramped quarters of the ordinary house, and it also saved firewood and candles, materials minded closely by thrifty Yankees.

Although a political conservative, President John Adams endorsed the liberal-minded custom of bundling. It was only practical, he thought. Adams, after all, had often contended with the rigors of a Massachusetts winter so severe that the ink froze in his pen while he was writing.

Unhappily, the Revolution did much to discourage the ingenious custom of bundling. As the Marquis de Barbe-Marbois explained, "The first French officers who were permitted it conducted themselves with so little reserve that the old people begged the mothers not to permit them this form of courtship with their daughters."

Colonial ladies were well skilled in the art of coquetry. Their armaments consisted of "ribands," "boskins," perfumes, sly winks and pretty ankles. They were, on the whole, very practical in their stratagems. For instance, here is sound advice from *The Ladies' Philosophy of Love* written in 1774:

All cheats of art reject with fierce disdain,
No cursed rouge thy tender cheek must stain.
No hot Arabian drug infect thy breath;
Deceit revealed to love is certain death.
Flee garlic, nuisance of Iberia's plains,
By HORACE curst in everlasting strains,
Mustard, on which th' unwary feeder raves;
Onions and leeks, the food of Hebrew slaves.

Every Rose Has Its Thorn *is the title of this drawing by C. G. Mercier after J. L. G. Ferris. Courtesy of The Library of Congress.*

The Washington Family, *painted by Edward Savage. Shown with George and Martha Washington are her two grandchildren, Eleanor Parke and George Washington Parke Custis, who were adopted by the general. Courtesy of The National Gallery of Art, Washington, D.C.*

Particularly in the southern colonies, where the practice of bundling did not prevail, a rare opportunity for courting was provided at the court days and rural fairs. In many cases, these were the only occasions that drew together families from disparate and distant districts. At these, the crowning social events of the season, several days were spent buying and selling livestock, bartering merchandise and awarding prizes to some goodwives' outstanding pickles and preserves.

Hearts were won and lost in country sporting events. There was wrestling, with hair pulling, eye gouging and ear biting standard procedure. There were horse races, foot races for each sex, greased pig chases, whistling and grinning matches. This last was a peculiar pastime whose popularity is difficult to fathom by another generation. The grinning match was performed by two or more people endeavoring to exceed each other in the distortion of their features, while every one of them had his head thrust through a horse collar.

Courtship practices have certainly changed since the eighteenth century, but there is one aspect of wooing that remains as difficult today as it was in colonial times: meeting the bride's father. Even two hundred years ago, a suitor approached his prospective father-in-law with gingerly reserve. And then, as now, a father was never prepared for *the* question. Certainly George Washington, the guardian of his niece Harriot, was unprepared for this letter in the midst of his run-of-the-mill correspondence:

Although entirely unknown to you, circumstances relative to your Niece, Miss Harriot Washington, and myself, make it necessary for me to trouble you with a letter, and to give you intimation of what has occurred between us. I have made my addresses to her and she has referred me to you, whose consent I am to acquire, or her objections to a Union with me are, I am afraid, insuperable. Having then no hope of possessing her unless I should be so fortunate as to obtain your assent, and as my happiness measurably depends upon your determination, I shall endeavor by stating to you my situation and prospects in life....

I have lived in Fredericksburg for more than three years. My connections generally reside in Baltimore, and are mostly rich. I am engaged here in the Mercantile Business and concerned therein with my Brother-in-Law, Mr. McElderry of Baltimore. My fortune at present does not much exceed three thousand pounds, but with industry and economy, I have every expectation of rapidly improving my condition in that respect....

I am, Sir, with infinite respect,
Your most obedient and humble servant,
/s/ Andrew Parks

A pastoral romantic scene sketched by Benjamin Latrobe in 1792.

Washstand, made of mahogany and built in about 1775. Courtesy of The Henry Francis du Pont Winterthur Museum.

Washington was taken aback. Aides-de-camp and cabinet officers were useless to him. He applied to Martha for help, and together they drafted a letter which said, in part, that money wasn't everything, that there were more important requisites, the happiness of his niece chief among them.

Since there was no F.B.I. in those days to check the credentials of Andrew Parks, Washington asked some friends in Fredericksburg to look into the young man's background. He particularly wanted to know whether Parks was "a native or a foreigner." Actually, Uncle George had been hoping for a match, "a better connection" as he called it, with the son of Marquis de Lafayette. Still, in the end, Harriot Washington was allowed to marry the man of her choice.

While we don't know much of the courtship of Harriot and Andrew Parks, we know that many young men and women were thrown together by the circumstances of the war, and that many a heart was won by the pleasant recollection of a roaring fire, a groaning board, savory hotchpot and a pretty girl in petticoats. Imagine this scene in a farm home in Pennsylvania. Martha Prouty is preparing to meet her dashing cousin David, who is a soldier in General Washington's army. The family is bustling about, getting ready for the event, and as for the young hero—he can't wait to tell his pretty relative about his exploits against the British.

A Visiting Hero

"Martha... Martha! Don't keep a-settin' there like a stump. Come in and help me. We Prouty women don't moon around. We get up and go it."

"Oh, Mama, I just hope he likes the house."

"Of course he will, child. It's as clean as whisk broom and vinegar wash can make it."

"But, Mama, he's a soldier in General Washington's army."

"That don't make no difference, Martha. Cousin Leighton is just a Hampshire man in uniform. Why up there in the New Hampshire grants, there's some of 'em what lives in holes in the ground. Besides, if he's been with the rebel army for even a year, you know he's a stranger to a warm hearth and home-cooked food."

"Well, I hope he's interested in something besides food."

"Nonsense. Now come help me set the tableboard. Use the linen cloth, not that old huckaback. And light the betty lamps."

"Shall I set with the porcelain cups or the pewter?"

"Pewter's perfectly good. Even that high muckety-muck John Hancock prefers pewter to porcelain. Besides, we haven't enough porcelain as it is, but I have the full garnish of pewter given to me on the day your father and I were married. It's been in the family for years."

"I know, Mama, you've told me again and again. Now tell me, why can't Joseph help us? I swear that boy is...."

"Martha, your brother *is* helping. He was all morning polishing my pewter with scouring rushes. He's coming in now. Go open the door for him; he's been a-leafing and his hands are full. You know I refuse to bake bread without a bed of oak leaves to rest the dough. Bring those leaves here, Joseph, and go get Patience to start the roasts. Martha, you had better get dressed before Cousin Leighton comes. Go on now. Joseph! Where is that creature?"

"Here, Mama. I hate to see you use Patience to run the turnspit."

"Why, child, that's what turnspit dogs are for. They couldn't do anything else with those squat little bodies and stubby little legs but run in a turnspit drum. Besides, what would your mother do? The roasts won't turn themselves, and I have my hands full stirring hotchpot."

"Where's Martha?"

"Why, I believe she's putting her face and lips in order for a conquest. Martha, can you hear me, child? Are you going to wear your chintz with the new linen apron or your pretty little white whim?"

"My whim! Mama! Look, I'm all dressed, and I declare, I do think it looks quite as nice as a First-day in town."

"Well, there's my little girl. Look at that purple and white striped Persian gown, that white petticoat, muslin apron, gauze cap and handkerchief— you're all grown up! Oh, here they come. Now, daughter, don't stare at Cousin Leighton. It's...it's *unmaidenly.*"

"Come in, David, and meet my family. Cousin Leighton, meet my wife and the children, Martha and Joseph. Now, how about a cider!"

"Heigh-ho, John Prouty; I'll thank you for one of your good Pennsylvania

Coffeepot (above) with the handle interestingly located on the side, and a candle mold (below), both objects commonly found in the colonial kitchen. Courtesy of The Concord Antiquarian Society.

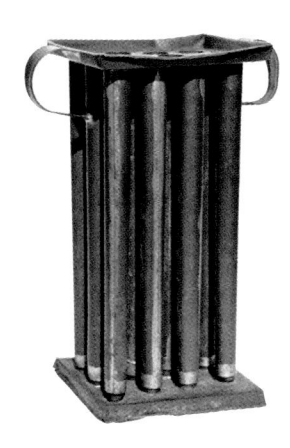

phlegm-cutters. I've drunk Quince in New York, Jersey Lightning and Stonewalls in New Hampshire — great inciters of riot and rebellion all — but give me Pennsylvania cider before a full meal."

"And such a meal! Come, bring your cider, David."

"Holy saints and virgin! Hot bread, pumpkin suppawn and milk, roast ducks and chicken, beef hotchpot, porter, beer, creams, custards, jellies, cheese, mince pie — a most sinful feast, Goodwife Prouty!"

"Is it somewhat different than your usual fare?"

"By the great horn spoon, my camp fare has been soup bones, potatoes, calf's foot, cabbage and sheep's nose — and that's when there was anything at all!"

"I most devoutly pray that all that hardship will change now!"

"Aye, John, another like the battle of Germantown and we'll be eating turkey and the Redcoats, crow."

"Were you there at Germantown?"

"Wasn't I though, Miss Martha. How do you think this militaryish coat became this devilish rag but from frowsting under rocks and bushes while we tore those Redcoats to pieces. Why, John Sullivan, his Hampshire boys and the rest of the militia struck straight down the Germantown Road into the core of the British strength. We cut 'em down like we was' flailing wheat. Right into town we came, lumbering through the fog with our cannon, bristling with musketry. Then out comes that pissgut British dandy William Howe, crying, 'For shame Light Infantry!…it's only a scouting party.' Then the fog cleared a moment and we loosed a hot hail of grapeshot on 'em. It rattled round Howe's ears like banshee devils, and believe me, he's never again going to mistake your Continental army for a scouting party!

"Damnation, we would have driven 'em all the way to Philadelphia if it hadn't been for some of our officers dillydallying to the rear at the Chew House."

"*Our* distinguished officers?"

"Listen, ma'am, the only thing distinguishing about our officers is that they wear socks and the rest of us don't. But I tell you, that Washington knows his trade. There were some who said he couldn't make decisions, and some what said he made wrong decisions. But not now. Not after Germantown. I say, 'God save great Washington, God damn the King!' "

"We'll drink to that, Cousin Leighton!"

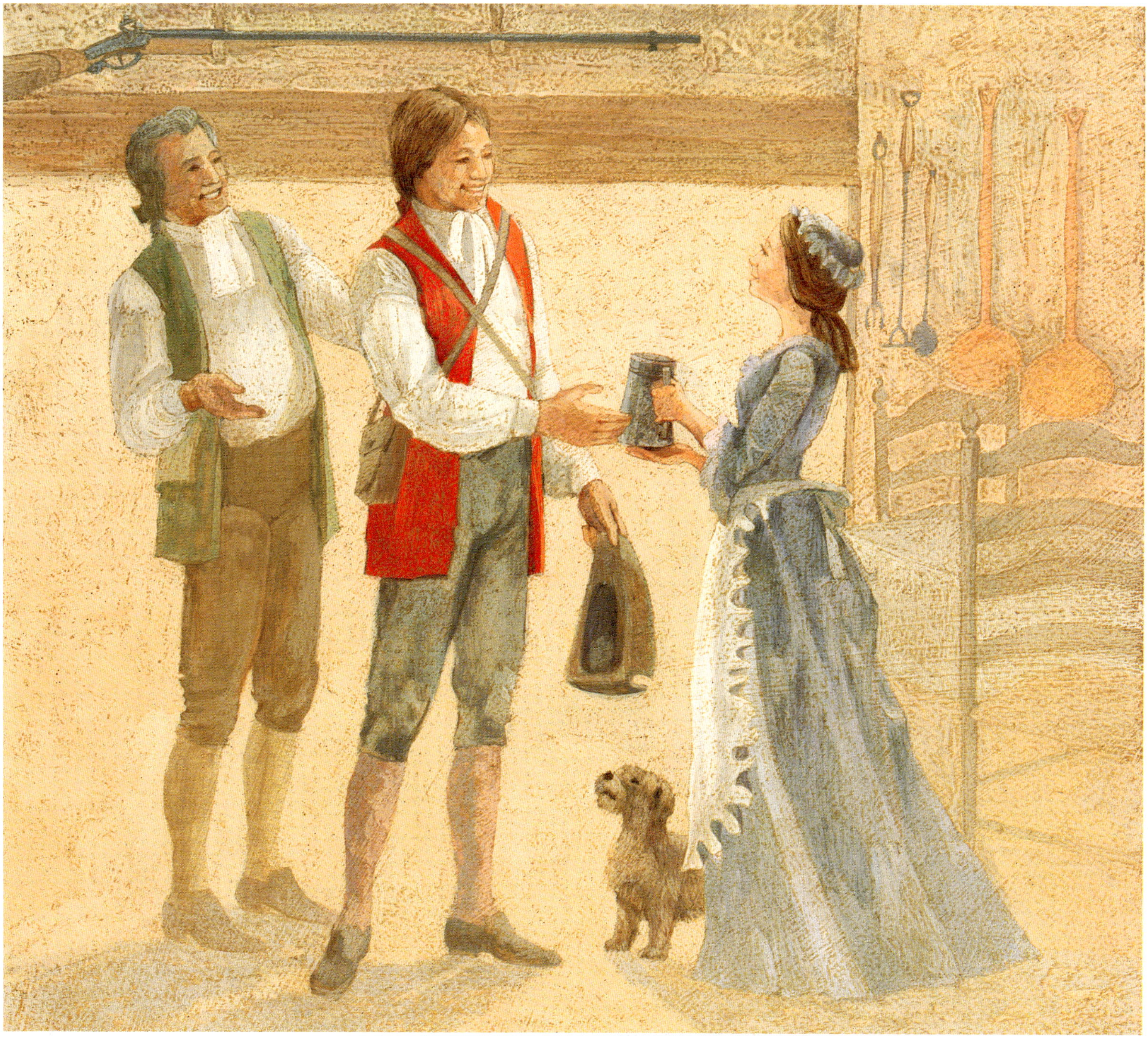

Discovering a New Identity

More important than a scenario for a young girl's first infatuation with a soldier in uniform, the conversation at the Prouty home illustrates further the change of heart in the colonies. Increasingly among the patriot faction, men and women discovered their identities as Americans rather than Englishmen, and they began to see themselves as members of a new nation, separate and apart.

Why was this so? The war itself accelerated the emergence of a new identity. Mobility was the key. Marylanders were brought face-to-face with Yankees from the New England states. Men from the frontier areas learned to respect the courtly men from the Carolinas and Virginia. Soldiers like David Leighton would find sweethearts in faraway colonies, and together, men and women would build a new national allegiance.

Private Joseph Plumb Martin of Connecticut heard a Pennsylvania woman say that her little girl had been so mischievous that she should be given to the Yankees. "Take care how you speak of the Yankees," said Martin's wagon mate. "I have one of them here." "Ha!" said the woman. "Is he a Yankee?...I don't see any difference between him and other people."

At the dawn of the Revolution, those purgatory days, recruits rebelled at fighting outside their home states, and some refused to serve under officers born in other regions. Washington had weathered the leadership crisis, and now the Continental army, such as it was, fought as a unit, its men swearing fealty to the concept of America, the nation.

Battles like Germantown were critical. This engagement, and smashing victories like Washington's Christmas drive across the Delaware to Trenton, showed the American army, demoralized under the bludgeon of repeated defeat, that the British were, in fact, mortal and fallible. Now they could almost taste victory.

The year of Germantown, 1777, was a milestone in another fashion as well. This was the year when the signers of the Declaration made known their names. In 1776, men knew that a Declaration of Independence had been passed over the signature of John Hancock, president of the Congress. But the next year was the point of no return, the year when the signers wagered their lives and sacred honor on the concept of an independent America.

It was a year that ended with a flowering of national optimism. But this, too, was a victory won not entirely on the battlefield, but in the minds of men. Independence seemed no distant dream when men could look at the American wilderness about them and boast, "Here, I made a home!"

Each colonist was a Robinson Crusoe, long schooled in relying on the virtues of individualism. Ours was a nation of Renaissance men—men like Franklin and Jefferson, who could turn with equal skill to many fields; men like Francis Hopkinson of New Jersey, one of the Declaration signers who was, by turns, a composer of cantatas and liturgical music, a writer of essays and verse, a practicing lawyer, professional artist and inventor and businessman. Even the ordinary John Proutys of the land were cast in the same mold. These sturdy farmers were at once wood-carvers, sheep shearers, hog butchers, broom makers, drovers and teamsters, makers of cartridge boxes and firearms, designers of canal locks, grinding mills and, lastly, they were sometime soldiers.

Americans like these, and generations of Americans to come, would draw sustenance from their bountiful land, measure their ambition against the virgin vistas, adopt the wilderness as a promise of manifest destiny.

And in 1777, manifest destiny meant nationhood.

Attack Upon the Chew House, *painted by Howard Pyle.*
The Americans' attempt to take the barricaded home of Tory Benjamin Chew away from the British was a strategic error that contributed greatly to an American defeat in the Battle of Germantown.
Courtesy of The Delaware Art Museum.

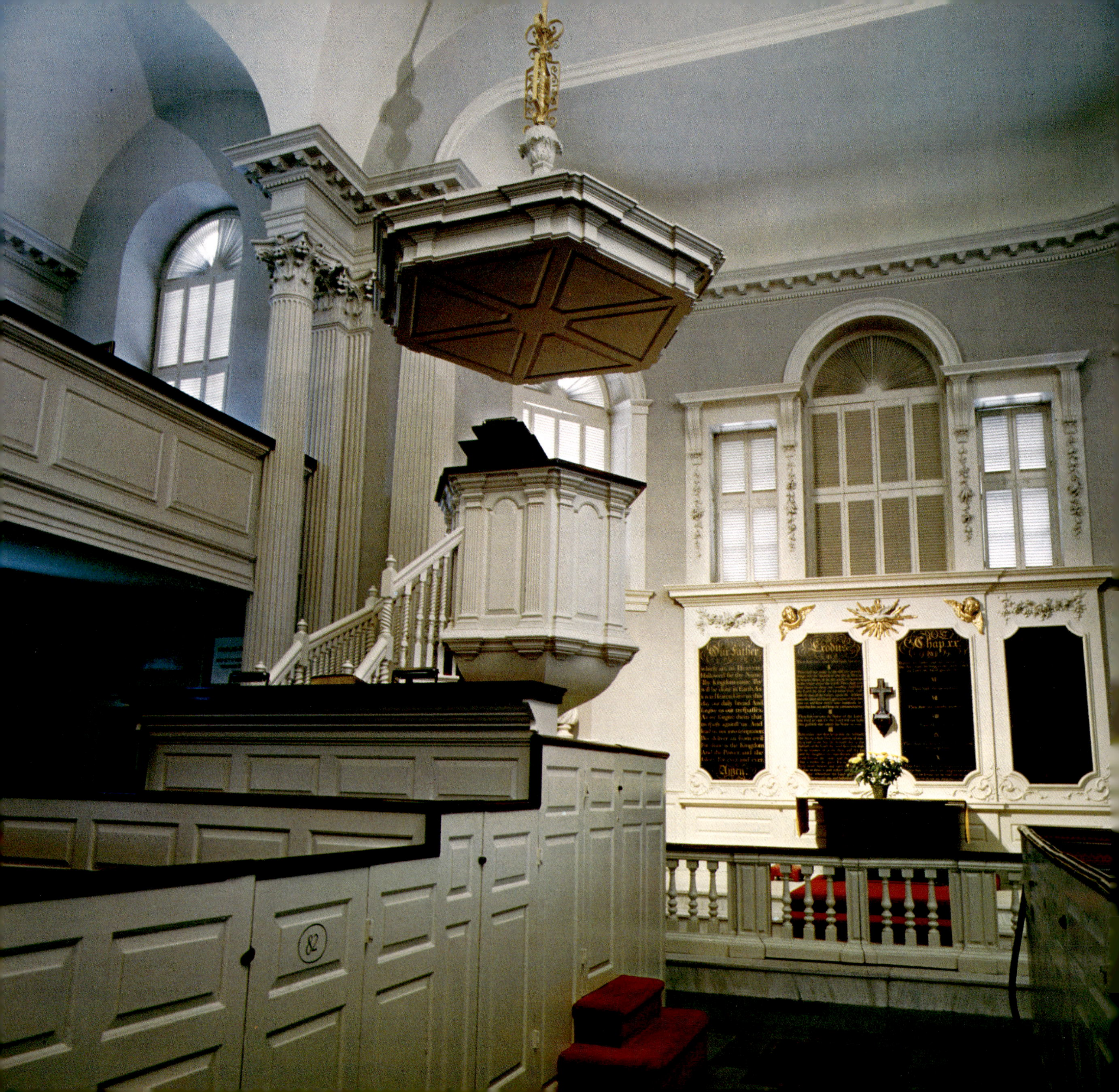
Our Father
Exodus
Chap. xx
Amen.
82

Chapter IV

THE REVOLUTION IN PULPIT AND PEW

The very first translation of any part of the New Testament in America was made by the Reverend Samuel Mather and printed in Boston in 1766. The title was "THE LORD'S PRAYER or, A New Attempt to recover the right Version, and genuine meaning of that Prayer."

Our Father, who art in the Heavens;
  sanctified be thy Name;
  Thy Kingdom come; Thy Will be, done,
  as in Heaven, so upon the Earth;
  Give us to Day that our Bread, the super-
    substantial;
  and forgive us our Debts,
  as we forgive them who are our Debtors;
  And introduce us not into afflictive Trial;
  but deliver us from the wicked One:
  Because thine is the Kingdom and the Power and
    the Glory for the Ages: Amen.

Does this not echo strangely in the mind? What a world of imagining it takes to recall a time when a fixture of everyday life like the Lord's Prayer, immutable as second nature, was spoken differently than today. Yet it was so among some Americans two hundred years ago.

Although its sound is as antique as the harpsichord, this was a landmark religious work that illustrates fundamental concepts in the eighteenth-century American mind. Here is a gingerly, painstaking effort to make God speak to ordinary people in the ordinary tongue. Here is the death and afterlife importance of religion made manifest in ten creaking lines.

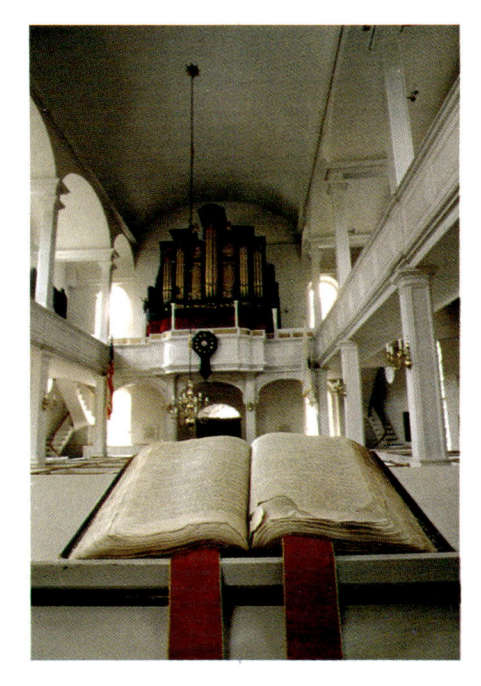

Pulpit Bible in Christ Church, Boston — also known as "Old North Church" — where signal lanterns were displayed in the steeple to indicate the positions of the British to Paul Revere.

King's Chapel, Boston. The building standing today was begun in 1749 on the site of the first chapel, built in 1688. The pulpit dates from 1717.

Old South Church, Boston, was built in 1730 and still stands today. It was here that, on June 14, 1768, John Hancock was appointed as a delegate to the governor to ask that the Boston port, which the British had closed, be reopened. The refusal of this request eventually led to the famous Boston Tea Party. Courtesy of The Library of Congress.

We talk a good deal about technology and its products, how our lives are changed by these products and how men of the past would marvel at our accomplishments. But, bring Franklin, Mather or any of the Founding Fathers back to earth today, and push-button radios and automobiles would not impress them half as much as the relative disappearance of religion from our lives.

In revolutionary America, the word of God was in every man's mouth. Religion was a burning issue in pulpit and politics both. There was a cerebral contest of wills between deism and orthodoxy. There were very material contests between individuals, as religious factions divided along class lines. There were bitter instances of prejudice and bigotry at the same time America embraced more varied and divergent religions than any other country on the globe, beginning an original and unusual experiment in toleration.

In the American wilderness of the eighteenth century, God seemed less distant and theoretical than today; His hand manifest in a land of hardship, superstition, uncertainty and sudden death. Spiritual tolerance was a difficult step, precisely because religion was so important. American faith was no matter of ethereal philosophy; it was robust, muscular stuff, hardy as the frontier.

A Minister and His Flock

Picture some Massachusetts family leaving behind a breakfast of wine and sugar rather than orange juice, of cold meat and porter instead of cornflakes on Sunday morning. Perhaps their town has no church bell. They are called to prayer, instead, by an elephantine blast on a giant conch, a drumbeat or musket shot. Soberly attired they march, elders first, children trailing, on a white highway of crushed seashells. Tarrying youngsters receive a silent rebuke as they pass a large cage set aside for the confinement of boys who do not properly observe the Sabbath.

Their church stands grim and gray beneath a copse of elms. Moss laps up on the sides where it is dark and damp. The meetinghouse door wears a beard of leaflets and papers: notices of town meetings, sales of cattle and land, lists of town officers, marriage bans. Further on, the gaunt, gray walls

Augustus Lutheran Church, Trappe, Pennsylvania, built in 1743, is the oldest Lutheran church in the United States and is an excellent example of the rural or "country" church.

are swabbed with blood and decorated with the fierce and grinning heads of wolves. The minister who guides this parish is, like as not, sunburned, rawboned and austere in his dark, severe, broadcloth suit. His hands are just as calloused as those of the farmers and shopkeepers — hardest working folk on earth. The devil hasn't a chance against this iron-willed man of God. His stern words never fail to guide his flock down the right path — or at least the direction he thinks they should go. The following conversation between the Reverend Mr. Morgus and some of his parishioners might have taken place on any Sunday in those event-filled days of the Revolution:

"Good day to you, Reverend Morgus!"
"Good morning, Ephraim, sister Sabry, Aaron and little Tabatha. You shan't this day profane the Sabbath, will you sister Tabatha?"
"No, sir."
"If I see further wicked behavior from you, Tabatha, I shall tell the tithing man to use such blows and prods as he deems necessary. Mind me now, no

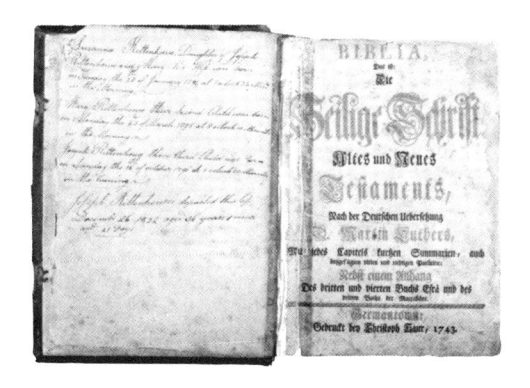

German Bible, printed in Germantown, Pennsylvania, by Christopher Saur in 1743. Courtesy of The Germantown Historical Society.

more of your wry faces that beget laughter and misbehavior in beholders."

"Oh, no, no, no. I'm a good girl, ain't I, Pa?"

"Perhaps not so good that the tithing man and his birch rod can't make you a better one. Run along with your mother now. Have you heard, Reverend Morgus, that the one they call John Wesley the Methodist has called upon the patriot Americans to lay down their arms and return like submissive children to the embrace of bloody England?"

"A curse upon these barbarous Methodists, Ephraim. They are no better than howling atheists. And I'll wager your John Wesley never had England's agents scouring his forests for the biggest, stoutest timbers for England's ships and leaving naught behind but saplings the bigth of a hemp rope. British prodigality hinders me from making ships, and British laws prevent my shipping cargoes."

"Aye, Reverend, there's a tax on this and a tax on that. Now there's John Bull's Liverpool pigs being quartered in our homes. Our daughters are not safe. Our food is not our own, the while the patriot army starves. How long, Reverend, how long are we to be so tormented!"

"Yonder on our wall you see the heads of twoscore wolves, and a fat bounty paid for each of the murderous rascals. There will come a day, Ephraim, when the heads of British infantry prove just as valuable. England had her chance at peace, and here we are at war. Was not Rehoboam of the Bible, son of Solomon, even like King George of England? When the children of Israel spoke to him and asked if it was not in his heart to ease their oppression and lift the yoke his father had set upon them, he answered, My little finger shall be thicker than my father's loins.... For whereas my father put a yoke upon you, I will put more to your yoke.... And when all Israel saw that the King would not hearken unto them, the people answered the King saying what portion have we in David? We have none. And they went thence to govern themselves. Then King Rehoboam sent Hadoram, that was over the tribute to tax the people, and the children of Israel stoned him with stones that he died. And Israel rebelled against the house of David unto this day."

"So it is written in the Bible, Reverend. And yet I wonder—can we win the rebellion?"

"I believe so, Ephraim. Every time the hinged pews of our flock slam down for prayer for deliverance from oppression, it sounds like musket fire to me, and I believe we shall win, Ephraim, I believe we shall."

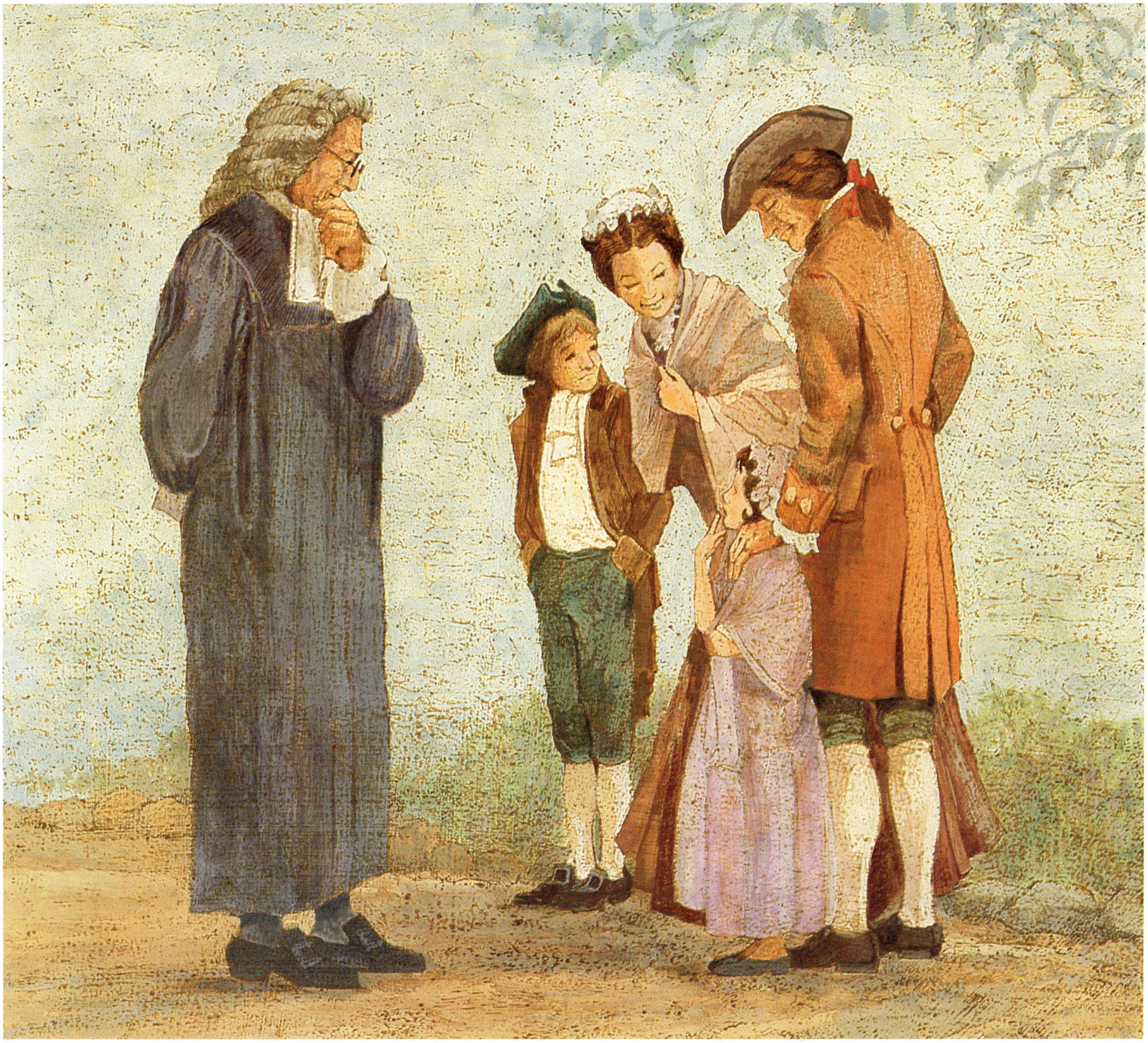

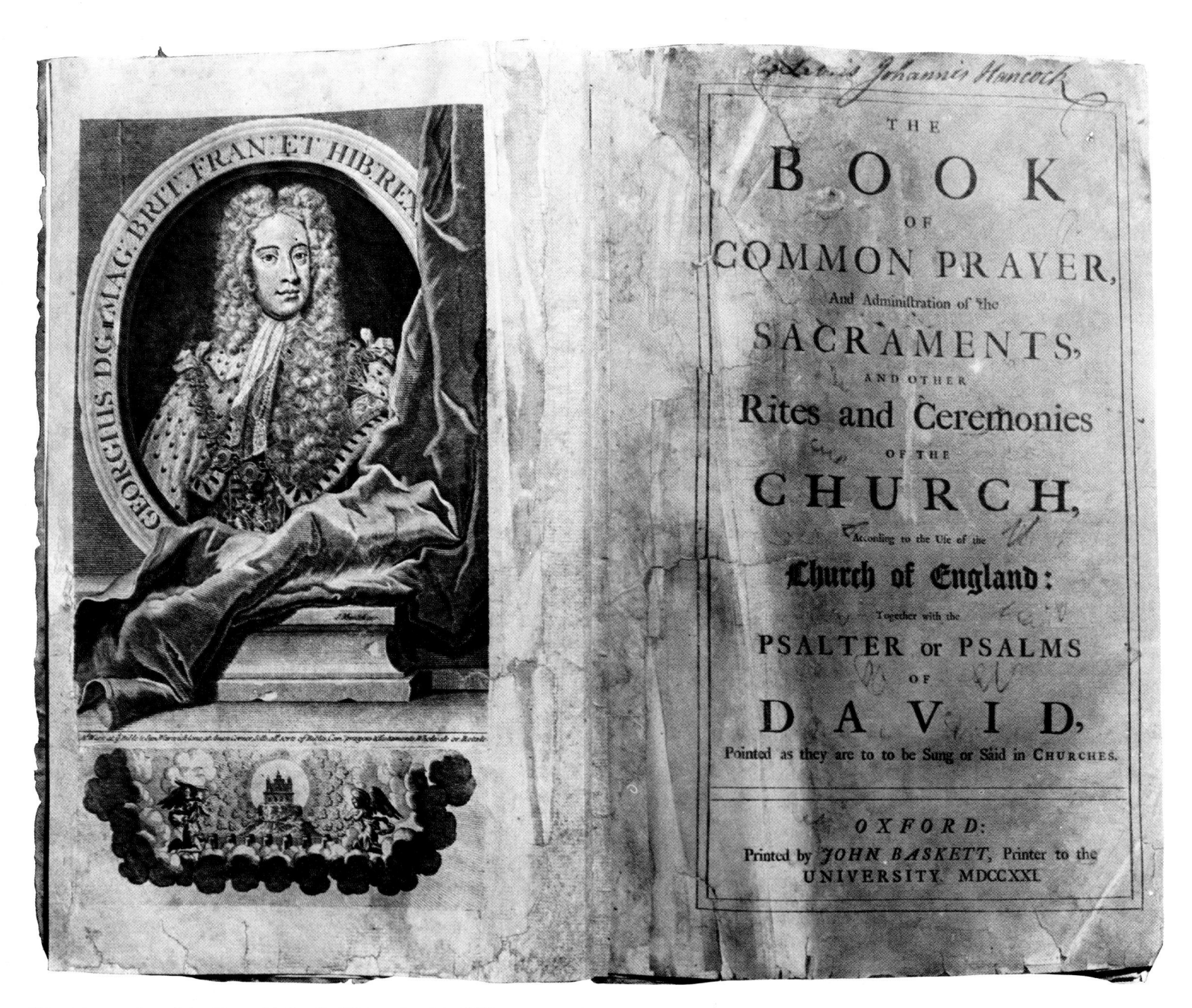

The title page from John Hancock's family Bible, printed in 1721, bears the signature of his father. Courtesy of The Bostonian Society.

So this was the kind of man who brought God to the people of many colonial communities: a bark-knuckled man of God who mixed the secular with the spiritual. Little different than his neighbors to whom he preached, he, too, felt England's hand in his pocket. He was, however, skilled in citing biblical support of his business interests, able in marshaling Kings and Chronicles to the defense of patriotism.

Preachers, Politics and Profits

"Congregationalists, Presbyterians and smugglers" are the foes of the English government, charged Joseph Galloway. His phrase recognizes the curious mixture of religious and business interests. Many ministers were farmers; others owned interests in mines and blast furnaces. Still others pursued unlikely careers outside the pulpit. As late as 1790, Dr. Nathan Strong, a fellow of Yale College, chaplain of Colonel Samuel Wylly's regiment in the Revolution and pastor of the first church in Hartford, carried on a distillery in partnership with his brother-in-law, within four hundred yards of the church. It was said that the pastor of West Hartford raised the rye which Strong distilled into whiskey which the minister at East Hartford drank.

The pastor with a vest-pocket business was in a sense playing a traditional role, and in a sense was a harbinger of the secularism to come. When a community was fashioned out of the wilderness, the minister was the first bloom of civilization to take root, even before the doctor, lawyer or schoolmaster, in whose place the minister often served. In fact, the Dutch church was served by an official called the *voorlezer* or chorister, who was also called upon to act as bell ringer, sexton, funeral inviter, schoolmaster and sometimes town clerk. All the manifold duties of the town clergyman contributed toward making him a considerable and powerful personage. The Reverend Samuel Phillips of Andover, Massachusetts, put it best. When asked whether he was "the parson who serves here," he thundered, "I am, Sir, the parson who rules here!"

What a champion such a man must have been on the side of liberty. Imagine him, invested with wealth, respect and lordly influence, surrounded in Sunday's pulpit by the almost palpable presence of divinity, there to trumpet the cause of revolution, buttressing his arguments with holy verse

Jonathan Mayhew
Courtesy of The Massachusetts Historical Society.

This window from the Augustus Lutheran Church has its original glass panes, through which another window on the opposite side of the church can be seen.

and scripture. Yes, the pulpit was one of the most important forces in the community for controlling and shaping public opinion, clearly on a par with taproom and tavern.

Nor did patriot parsons hesitate to raise their voices against the king. The Reverend John H. Weikel courted disaster when he preached on the text "Better is a poor and wise child, than an old and foolish King, who will no more be admonished." Then Jonathan Mayhew told his Boston congregation in 1776 that "wise, brave and virtuous men were always friends to liberty; that God gave the Israelites a King, or absolute monarch, in His anger, because they had not sense and virtue enough to like a free commonwealth."

The clergy, too, felt the spirit of manifest destiny abroad in their new land. Their clamorous nationalism was nourished in the conviction that God Himself guided their adventure in the wilderness. No wonder that Tory partisans complained that politics was their Gospel, that New England ministers were wicked, malicious and inflammatory, their pulpits "converted into Gutters of Sedition."

The vigorous proselytizing of patriot ministers became an indefatigable propaganda machine for keeping troops in the field. Clergymen were attached to Washington's staff simply to urge reenlistment among recruits, whose prescribed term of service was often a ridiculously scant sixty days.

Meanwhile, ministers on the home front beat the bushes for willing recruits. John Cleaveland of Ipswich persuaded his entire parish to enlist and then volunteered himself. David Avery of Windsor, Vermont, getting wind of patriot bloodshed at Lexington and Concord, preached a sermon in which he called his congregation to arms. He then bade his flock farewell and marched away at the head of a score of volunteers.

Some ministers served as chaplains and some as common soldiers. Some, though loathe to bear arms and violate the first commandment, would not stand idly by and see the cause of liberty so heartily embraced by friends and neighbors come to ruin. Take the example of intrepid James Caldwell of the Presbyterian church of Elizabeth, New Jersey. When the American militia ran out of wadding for their muskets during the battle of Springfield, Caldwell opened his church, scooped up armfuls of *Watts' Psalm Book*s and dashed back to the front lines, tossing psalms to the militiamen and exhorting them, "Now, boys, give 'em Watts! Give 'em Watts!"

Interior of the Augustus Lutheran Church (left) and (above and below) details of the stairway leading to the gallery. All the timbers used were hewn, framed with tenons and unpainted.

Interior of the Independent Presbyterian Church (above), Savannah, Georgia. This church was destroyed by fire in 1889, but an exact replica of the original was built and still stands today. Courtesy of The Library of Congress.

St. John's Church, Richmond, Virginia. It was here, on March 20, 1775, that Patrick Henry delivered a speech concerning the need to arm for war and uttered the words that were to stir generations of Americans: "Give me liberty or give me death!"

Religion in the South

Outside of the northern tier of provinces, clerical support of the rebellion wavered. In the South, a stronghold of Anglicanism, there was considerable restive loyalty to the crown. Because of his outspoken support of the Loyalist cause, the Reverend Jonathan Boucher of Virginia deemed it prudent to preach with a brace of loaded pistols before him on a pillow. Sometimes we misconstrue the Revolution as a genteel contest between men in powdered wigs and satin breeches. It was no such thing. It was as grim and desperate as the Frontier West or any other period in American history. One bright Sunday morning, armed men stormed in on Boucher's worship service and dragged him bodily from his church.

Boucher was persecuted because of his Tory principles. Yet there were many other churchmen reviled simply because, as British castoffs, drunkards and felons, they were loathsomely inadequate as ministers. These did the Loyalist cause no good whatsoever.

Although by reputation the Southern church was distinguished for its libertine parishioners and less than saintly ministers, the blandishments of material over spiritual pursuits ruined many a clergyman, north and south. Ministers proved so bad a morality risk in the middle states that in 1771 a colonial assembly passed a law subjecting pastors to special scrutiny.

The passage of time wrought changes in the minister's position as secular interests absorbed the population. Between 1700 and the time of the Revolution, at least forty-eight preachers in New England had to sue their parishioners for unpaid salaries. The deterioration of public esteem for the clergy was one of the steps toward revolution, for it made the rejection of other figures of authority, chiefly British, appear eminently reasonable.

The difference between the church philosophies of Josiah Quincy in the North and William Byrd in the South was sometimes apparent in colonial church decor. The churches of the Southern colonies were, as a rule, much more richly furnished and frequently festooned with flowers.

Jonathan Boucher described the greater number of Southern churches at the time of the Revolution as "composed of wood, without spires, or towers or steeples or bells, placed in retired and solitary spots and contiguous to springs or wells." While the churches of the South were elaborate and steepleless, those of New England remained bare and prosaic save for a soaring flourish of brilliant ecclesiastical architecture in the steeple.

A Potpourri of Faiths

America's multiplicity of sects did not necessarily guarantee forbearance. James Madison, "learning that not less than five or six Baptists" were held "in close jail" in the winter of 1774, protested that the "hell-conceived principle of persecution rages among some." Charges and countercharges filled the air.

Toleration remained frail and brittle for many years. Ideologies were fanatically espoused. Franklin said the hurly-burly of religious discussion reminded him of "a certain French lady," who, in a dispute with her sister, said, "I don't know how it happens, sister, but I meet with nobody but myself that's always in the right."

Bruton Parish Church, Williamsburg, Virginia, has been in use continuously since 1715. In prerevolutionary times, church and state were united in Virginia, obliging by law all officeholders to attend church regularly.

Often, religious factions paralleled class lines and political sentiments. Lower-class republican farmers were often drawn to the Methodist and Anabaptist sects, whose emotional services represented the zenith of participatory religion. Gentlemanly Thomas Jefferson, who was branded "a howling atheist," accepted a deistic philosophy. He was thought to be a dangerous radical and was much feared by John Adams and those politically conservative Americans who also favored strict, unadulterated Calvinism.

Indeed, there are many Americans today who would find Jefferson's religious beliefs somewhat disconcerting, for he rejected the Immaculate Conception of Jesus, His deification, corporeal presence in the Eucharist, the Trinity and original sin. And in 1796, there were many who agreed with the sentiments of the Connecticut minister who prayed for the newly elected vice-president, saying, "O Lord! Wilt Thou bestow upon the Vice President a double portion of Thy grace, for *Thou knowest he needs it.*"

Even George Washington, by no means a dangerous radical, chose to go his own way in these matters of conscience. One Sunday in Philadelphia, Dr. James Abercrombie of Christ Episcopal Church sought to rebuke the president for habitually leaving before the celebration of Communion. Abercrombie lectured on the grave responsibility of "those in elevated stations" to set a good example. The object of his remarks was clear to every nervous, anguished body in the pews. This public reprimand must have stung Washington considerably, but the result was not entirely satisfactory from Abercrombie's point of view. True—Washington never again left church before the Lord's Supper; in fact, thenceforth on Communion Sundays, he never showed up at all.

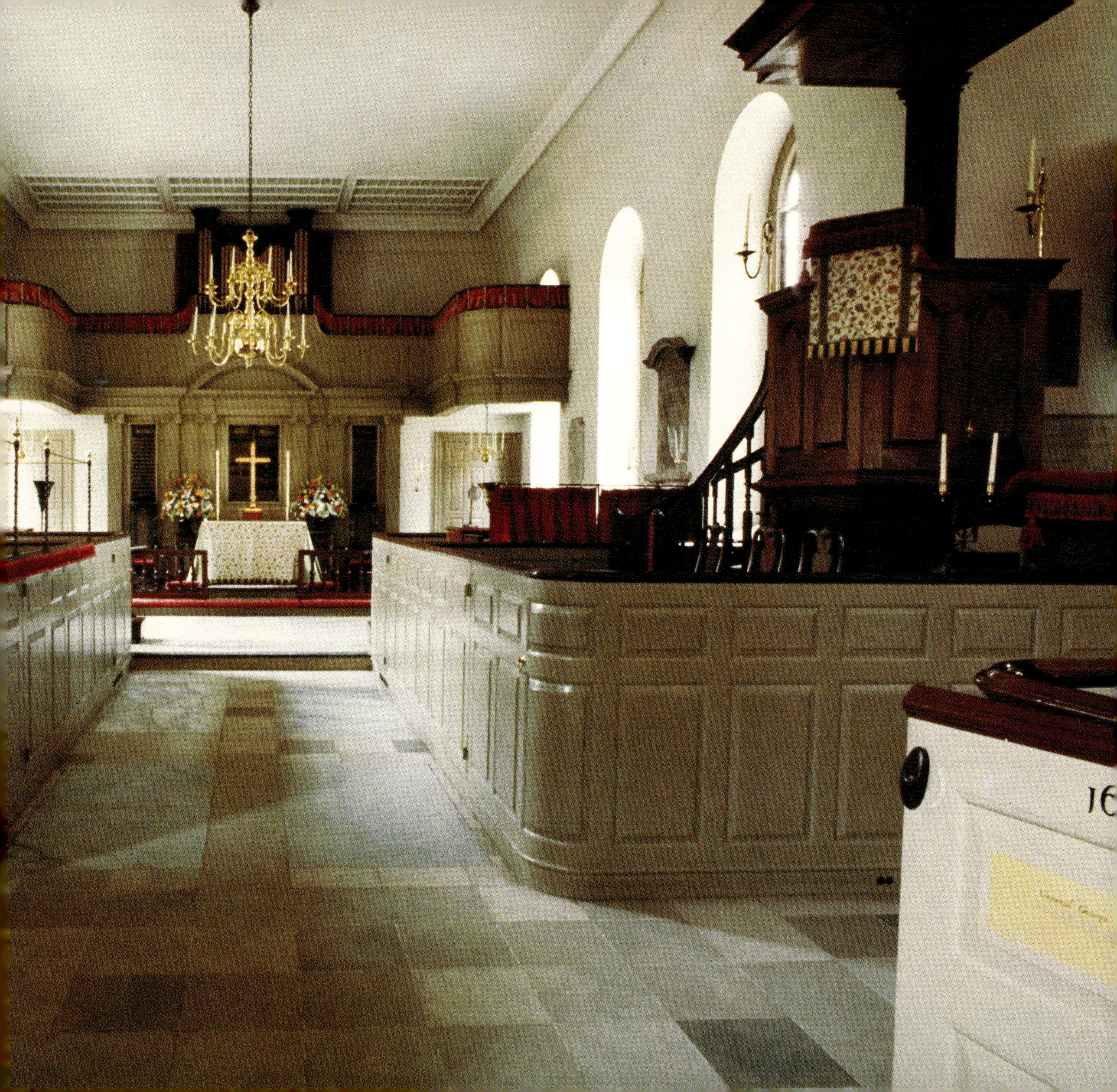
General George

Christ Church, Philadelphia, as seen in a 1787 engraving. On July 4, 1776, the bells of this church pealed forth in celebration of the signing of the Declaration of Independence. Courtesy of The Library of Congress.

What made the attitude of rationalists Jefferson and Washington the more remarkable was the pervasive opinion among ordinary Americans that theirs was a meddling deity, one who authored floods, earthquakes, good harvests and, presumably, the success of the Revolution. In Bennington Church, where the Reverend Jedediah Dewey preached a sermon of thanksgiving to God on the capture of Fort Ticonderoga, Ethan Allen, the flesh-and-blood hero of the battle, found himself consigned to a woefully insignificant role. Dewey droned on with unremitting humility and intermingled thanks for divine intervention at Ticonderoga. At last, Ethan complained aloud, "Aren't you going to mention the fact that I was there?" To which Dewey, at the head of the congregation, returned, "Ethan Allen, thou great infidel, sit down and be quiet!" The consensus was to give credit where credit was due; Ethan Allen was irrelevant.

From men like Washington and Jefferson, who made their own private decisions about God, to regional and class differences in worship, America was a tumult of individual views and expression. Antoine de Savanin discovered that even members of the same family might be of different persuasions. No one in the eighteenth-century world had ever before seen anything like the muddle of religious beliefs that was America. Just as the dangers of the revolutionary war taught men from Maryland and Delaware, New Hampshire and New York to reconcile their differences in the interests of achieving a great end, so there came a war on the devil that brought cohesion to America's diversity of views. The so-called Great Awakening at mid-century was the first universal, spontaneous movement in the history of the American people. It swept irresistibly from town to town, leaving in its wake free-lance ministries, a revulsion for formalism and pedantry and a newfound rapport between the colonies.

The evangelist George Whitefield touched the new sense of unity in this imaginary dialogue with Abraham, delivered before a Philadelphia congregation:

"Father Abraham, who have you in heaven? Any Episcopalians?"

"No."

"Any Presbyterians?"

"No."

"Any Baptists?"

"No."

"Any Methodists, Seceders, or Independents?"

"No, no!"

"Why, who have you there?"

"We don't know those names here. All who are here are Christians."

When the Revolution came, England wanted to know "who are those upstart rebels?" Edmund Burke told Parliament that Americans were chiefly Dissenters from the Church of England, accustomed to the freest discussion of all religious questions and extreme individualism. He said the right of private judgment in spiritual matters, the right to elect and dismiss religious leaders had been carried over into American politics. Edmund Burke was right.

George Washington
Courtesy of The Yale University
Art Gallery.

Thomas Jefferson
Courtesy of The Independence
National Historical Park Collection.

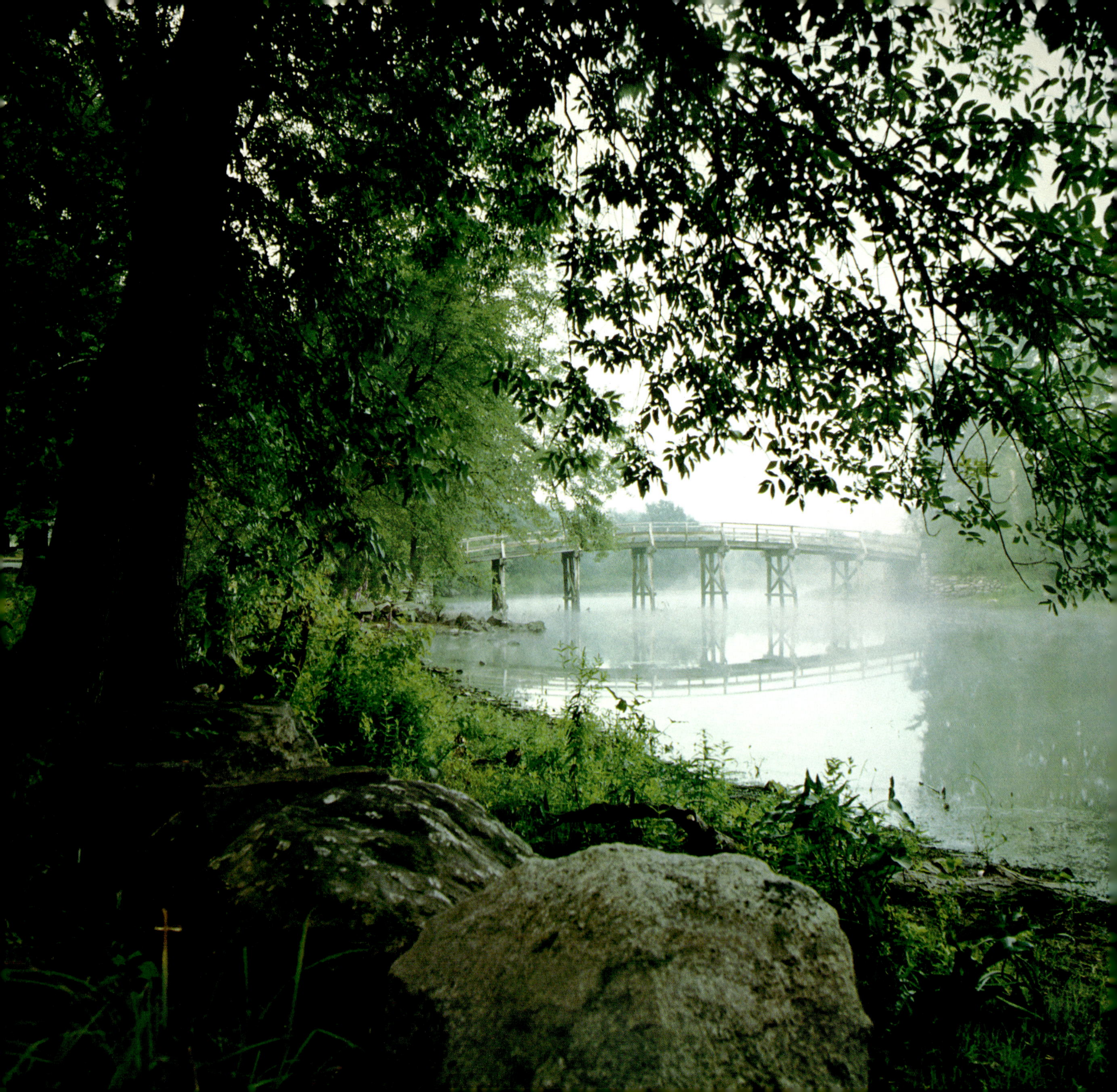

Chapter V

THE FIGHT FOR FREEDOM

A year had passed since the First Continental Congress in Philadelphia. Fall had turned to spring when, like some lush, fantastic flower of the new year, the British army appeared over the Concord hills. What had first caught the eye of local minutemen as a bud of distant color blossomed rank and file into a gaudy blaze of black coats, white coats, dark blue and sky blue coats, orange and buff and yellow, all laced and arabesqued and chevroned.

The British took Concord, detailing three companies to hold the North Bridge. Meanwhile, American companies from Concord, Lincoln, Chelmsford, Carlisle and Acton elbowed and jostled on the hilltop muster field. Animated by an edgy, bristling energy, the American militia hardly looked the part of heroes. They were drab, ragged and scared. Graybeard grandfathers coughed and wheezed with smooth-cheeked boys, wolfish malcontents spoiling for a fight, and wide-eyed, wan shopkeepers fingering rusty muskets. It was men like these that would drive Washington to inspired expostulation. "Never such a rabble dignified by the name of army!"

There was no question that these men felt overmatched and equally as inept as their house-and-garden weaponry. But this once at least, in Concord, courage was only fear that had said its prayers. A wisp of smoke drifted up and smiled lazily in the April sky and for the unblooded American army, push had come to shove. "They've put Concord to the torch!" terrified the minds of these husbands and fathers. The American militia gathered itself and rattled down the hill, an antique army of cold hands and quaking hearts.

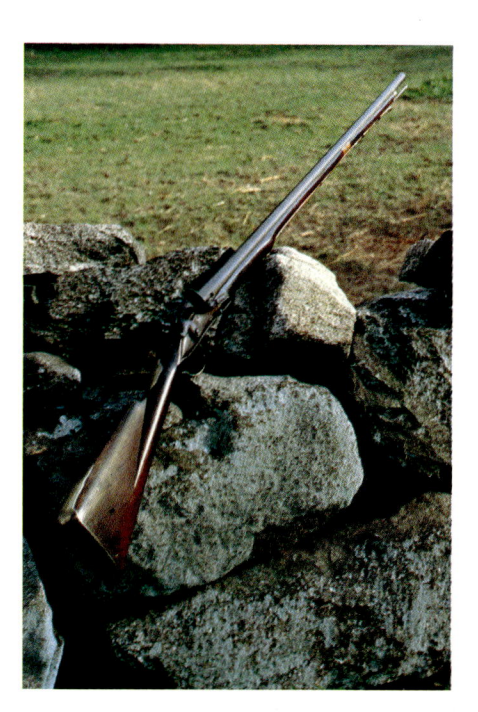

Musket used in the Battle of Concord. Courtesy of The Concord Antiquarian Society.

Concord Bridge, Concord, Massachusetts.

The Fight on Lexington Common (above), painted by Howard Pyle. Courtesy of The Delaware Art Museum. The front page of The Pennsylvania Gazette *(opposite), published in Philadelphia, was filled with signed eyewitness accounts of the "late hostilities in the province of Massachusetts Bay." Courtesy of The American Antiquarian Society.*

At the North Bridge, Britain's crack light infantry stood amazed as the rattle-gab of musket-bearing men poured off the hills. The British deployed for street fighting and strafed the Americans with ragged, hesitant fire, as if reluctant to engage this apocalyptic vision.

"It is strange there warn't no more killed," militiaman Amos Barrett was later to say, "but they fired too high."

Doggedly onward came the ragtag waves of militia. Then, inexplicably, the British broke and fled, panic-stricken, back from the bridge to Concord.

The American army pulled up short in wonderment and thanksgiving. "What had God wrought?"

The British regrouped and shortly appeared, ordered, groomed, chevroned and arabesqued once more, quitting Concord in lockstep. They funneled through files of American militia, sprouting thick as briers on the roadside. Then, in the midst of this tinder-tight, untenable position, a British company wheeled and fired a farewell volley.

The result was a veritable furnace of musketry. Ancient fowling pieces and heirloom muskets clanked into the rock vices of Concord's stone walls and spat and roared and ravaged. The terror of that situation is not to be imagined. British soldiers: running a gauntlet of hellfire, sulphur and smoke. Americans: pointing guns for the first time at men like themselves, so close you could search their faces, firing heavy, soft lead balls that would blow away a man's side.

It was an ugly thing. The British were hounded and harried from Concord to Menotomy, on toward Cambridge and Somerville. Men came, emptied their powder on the British and went home. Still more men came. Miraculously, only 72 English troops were killed out of 2,000.

The Americans were not superior marksmen. They were ruefully inept. It was as if you and your neighbors, schoolteachers, insurance salesmen, doctors, postmen and pharmacists were given guns today and asked to muster on Main Street to meet the national army of the Soviet Union. The expectations were the same. What was remarkable, truly remarkable, was that so many Americans thought that what had taken shape in Philadelphia a year before was worth dying for.

News of the bloodshed at Lexington and Concord spread southward with frightening speed. Colonel Joseph Palmer of Braintree got wind of the clash of arms and jotted down a terse alarm to the network of Committees of

May 17, 1775. **Numb. 2421.**

The Pennsylvania Gazette.

Containing the Freshest Advices, Foreign and Domestic.

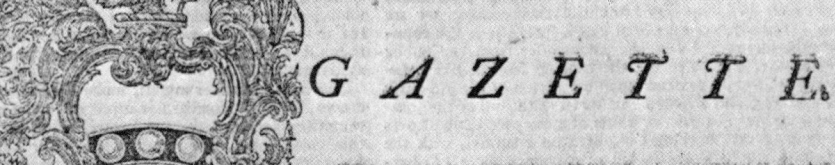

SWEET OIL, in Quarter Casks and Half Boxes; soft shelled Almonds, Walnuts, Jamaica Spirit, Sugar, old Lisbon Wine, of an excellent Quality; Brimstone, by the Hogshead, &c. &c.
TO BE SOLD, BY
CHARLES WHARTON,
At his STORE, near the DRAWBRIDGE.

JOSEPH VANDERGRIFF,
At the CROSS KEYS, the Corner of Chesnut and Third-streets,
PHILADELPHIA,
BEGS Leave to acquaint the Public in general, and his Friends in particular, that he has lately erected a LIVERY STABLE and CARRIAGE HOUSE, on Dock-street, between Second and Third-streets, near the City Tavern, having Conveniency for sixty Horses. He hopes to give Satisfaction to those that will favour him with their Custom, and will gratefully acknowledge their Favours.

TO BE SOLD,
THE Time of an indented SERVANT GIRL, who has between 3 and 4 Years to serve; she will suit very well for the Country, and will be sold at a reasonable Price. Enquire of OWEN BIDDLE.

FOR SALE,
A PLEASANT RETREAT, where the Subscriber now lives, on the Bank of Delaware, in the City of Burlington.——The premises consist of several lots of ground, on one of which is erected a good two story brick house, about 47 feet in front and 35 feet in depth, has 4 rooms on the first floor and six on the second, five of which are handsome chambers; contiguous to the house there is a neat milk-house, barn, stables, cow-houses, and sundry other useful buildings; also two gardens, well improved with a curious collection of choice fruit, such as pears, plumbs, cherries, apricots, peaches, &c. This lot is 200 feet front on Delaware, extends back to Pearl-street, and is enclosed with a cedar board fence. One other lot, near the aforesaid lot, contains one acre and a half, the chief of which is under good grass, and has a large cyder-mill and screw-press built upon it, with a house to cover them. The other land contains about 34 acres, ten of which is good meadow, six of orchard, and the residue plough land, which is also improved by an orchard of about 600 grafted apple-trees, that were planted this spring. Any person disposed to buy the premises aforesaid, or the house and part of the land, may know the terms, by applying to the subscriber, who will make the payments easy, upon his receiving security and interest for the principal.
Tbcrf. BENJAMIN SWETT.

TO avoid giving Offence, the MANAGERS of WICACOA MEADOWS thought it might be convenient to inform such Owners, as are unacquainted, or have forgotten what the Fines are that our Company are subject to by Law, for Non-payment of Taxes or Assessments, by inserting so much of the Law as relates thereto, to prevent as much as possible the Penalties for Non-compliance. ROBERT CORREY, Treasurer.
"And in case any of the said Owners, Occupiers, or Possessors aforesaid, shall refuse or neglect to pay, or cause to be paid, to the Treasurer aforesaid, on the Days and Times aforesaid, the several Sums of Money, which they respectively ought to pay or deposite, according to the true Intent and Meaning of this Act, they and each of them, so neglecting and refusing, shall forfeit and pay to the said Treasurer the additional Sum of Two Pence for every Shilling unpaid, which they respectively ought to have paid, by the Direction of this Act; and afterwards shall, for every Three Months Neglect or Refusal, in like Manner forfeit and pay to the Treasurer for the Time being, the like Sum of Two Pence for every Shilling which he, the

PHILADELPHIA.

AFFIDAVITS and depositions relative to the commencement of the late hostilities in the province of Massachusetts-Bay, together with an ADDRESS from the Provincial Convention of said province, to the inhabitants of Great-Britain, transmitted to the CONGRESS now sitting in this city, and published by their order.
CHARLES THOMSON, *Secretary.*

Lexington, April 25, 1775.

WE Solomon Brown, Jonathan Loring, and Elijah Sanderson; all of lawful age, and of Lexington, in the county of Middlesex, and colony of the Massachusetts-Bay in New-England, do testify and declare, that on the evening of the 18th of April instant, being on the road between Concord and Lexington, and all of us mounted on horses, we were about ten of the clock, suddenly surprized by nine persons, whom we took to be regular officers, who rode up to us mounted and armed, each having a pistol in his hand, and after putting pistols to our breasts, and seizing the bridles of our horses, they swore that if we stirred another step, we should be all dead men, upon which we surrendered ourselves; they detained us until two o'clock the next morning, in which time they searched and greatly abused us, having first enquired about the Magazine at Concord, whether any guards were posted there, and whether the bridges were up, and said four or five regiments of Regulars would be in possession of the stores soon——they then brought us back to Lexington, cut the horses bridles and girths, turned them loose, and then left us. *Solomon Brown, Jonathan Loring, Elijah Sanderson.*

Lexington, April 25, 1775.

I Elijah Sanderson, above named, do further testify and declare, that I was on Lexington common the morning of the 19th of April aforesaid, having been dismissed by the officers abovementioned, and saw a large body of regular troops advancing towards Lexington company, many of whom were then dispersing——I heard one of the regulars whom I took to be an officer say, "damn them we will have them," and immediately the regulars shouted aloud, run and fired on the Lexington company, which did not fire a gun before the regulars discharged on them. Eight of the Lexington company were killed, while they were dispersing, and at a considerable distance from each other, and many wounded, and although a spectator, I narrowly escaped with my life. *Elijah Sanderson.*

Lexington, April 23, 1775.

I Thomas Rice Willard, of lawful age, do testify and declare, that being in the house of Daniel Harrington, of said Lexington, on the 19th instant, in the morning, about half an hour before sunrise, looked out at the window of said house and saw (as I suppose) about 400 regulars, in one body, coming up the road, and marched towards the north part of the common, back of the meeting-house of said Lexington, and as soon as said regulars were against the east end of the meeting-house, the commanding officer said something, what I know not, but upon this the regulars ran till they came within about 8 or 9 rods of about 100 of the militia of Lexington, who were collected on said common, at which time the militia of Lexington dispersed, then the officers made a huzza, and the private soldiers succeeded them: Directly after this an officer rode before the regulars to the other

ordered our militia to disperse, and not to fire; immediately said troops made their appearance and rushed furiously, fired upon and killed 8 of our party, without receiving any provocation therefor from us. *John Parker.*

Lexington, April 24, 1775.

I John Robins, being of lawful age, do testify and say, that on the nineteenth instant, the company under the command of Capt. John Parker being drawn up (sometime before sunrise) on the green or common, and I being in the front rank, there suddenly appeared a number of the King's troops, about a thousand, as I thought, at the distance of about 60 or 70 yards from us, huzzaing, and on a quick pace towards us, with three officers in their front on horseback, and on full gallop towards us, the foremost of which cried, "throw down your arms, ye villains, ye rebels," upon which said company dispersing, the foremost of the three officers ordered their men, saying, "fire, by God fire," at which moment we received a very heavy and close fire from them, at which instant being wounded, I fell, and several of our men were shot dead by me; Captain Parker's men, I believe, had not then fired a gun: And further the deponent saith not.
John Robins.

Lexington, April 25, 1775.

We Benjamin Tidd, of Lexington, and Joseph Abbot, of Lincoln, in the county of Middlesex, and colony of Massachusetts-Bay in New-England, of lawful age, do testify and declare, that on the morning of the 19th of April instant, about 5 o'clock, being on Lexington common, and mounted on horses, we saw a body of regular troops marching up to the Lexington company, which was then dispersing, soon after the regulars fired first a few guns, which we took to be pistols from some of the regulars who were mounted on horses, and then the said regulars fired a volley or two, before any guns were fired by the Lexington company; our horses immediately started and we rode off, and further say not.
Benjamin Tidd, Joseph Abbot.

Lexington, April 25, 1775.

We Nathaniel Mullekin, Philip Russell, Moses Harrington, jun. Thomas and Daniel Harrington, William Grimes, William Tidd, Isaac Hastings, Jonas Stone, jun. James Wyman, Thaddeus Harrington, John Chandler, Joshua Reed, jun. Joseph Simonds, Phineas Smith, John Chandler, jun. Reuben Lock, Joel Viles, Nathan Reed, Samuel Tidd, Benjamin Locke, Thomas Winship, Simeon Snow, John Smith, Moses Harrington, the 3d, Joshua Reed, Ebenezer Parker, John Harrington, Enoch Willington, John Hormer, Isaac Green, Phineas Stearns, Isaac Durant and Thomas Headley, jun. all of lawful age, and inhabitants of Lexington, in the county of Middlesex, and colony of the Massachusetts-Bay in New-England, do testify and declare, that on the 19th of April instant, about one or two o'clock in the morning, being informed that several officers of the regulars had the evening before been riding up and down the road, and had detained and insulted the inhabitants passing the same: And also understanding that a body of regulars were marching from Boston towards Concord, with intent (as it was supposed) to take the stores belonging to the colony in that town, we were alarmed, and having met at the place of our company's parade were dismissed by our Captain, John Parker, for the present, with orders to be ready to

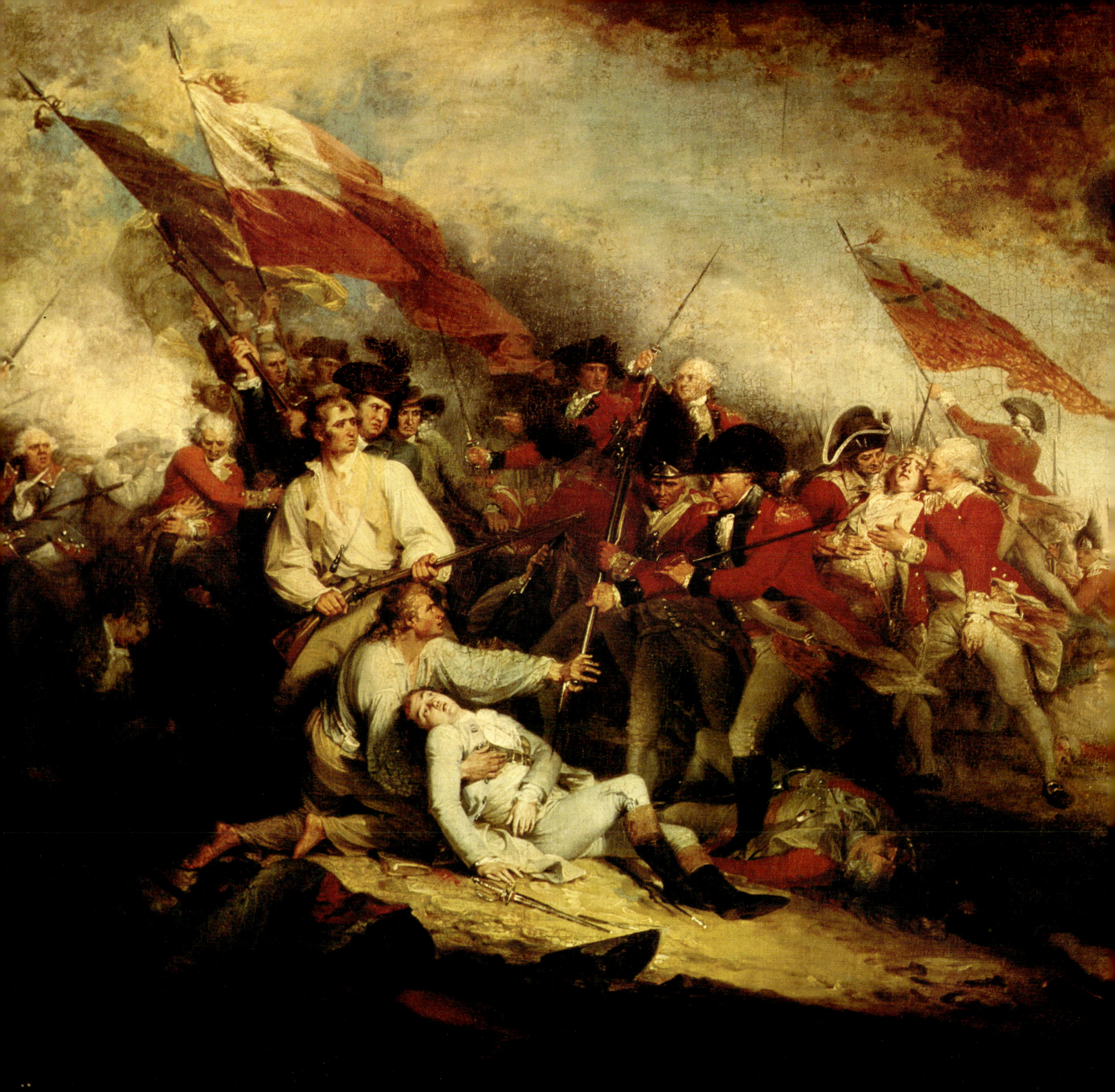

Safety throughout Massachusetts and Connecticut.

Israel Bissel, a good man on a fast horse, was tapped to carry the alarm. Not content with riding "quite to Connecticut," he turned his froth-flecked mount westward toward New York, crying his news on tavern stoops and village greens.

Four days after the first shot at Lexington, Bissel was in New York, mobbed by ragtag pariahs and town fathers clamoring to hear the news. Six days after, the forest broke away in front of him and Bissel pounded into Germantown, Pennsylvania.

Onward to Philadelphia. Ever southward the news sped with fateful urgency. Other hands, shaking with tension, added dramatic postscripts to Palmer's alarm, as if the force of words alone would eat up the miles. "Forwarded to Col. Thomas Couch…he to forward to Tobias Randolph, head of Elk, Maryland." "For God's sake send the man on without the least delay." "For the good of our Country, and the welfare of our lives and liberties and fortunes, you will not lose a moment's time."

By sea and land, the news hurried until, by May 8, the alarm sounded in the faraway accents of Charleston, South Carolina. The colonies were at war.

Americans Side by Side

No sooner had the winds of war broken upon villages and towns in the hinterland than these marshaled their menfolk and sent them trooping north to the siege of British Boston. Jesse Lukens came up with Colonel William Thompson's battalion of riflemen, there to forge a national army. Soon he was writing home, "Such Sermons, such Negroes, such Colonels, such Boys, & such Great Great Grandfathers."

Yes, young and old and, from the very beginning, black troopers manned the Continental Line. This caused some discussion, especially in the South, but it was generally agreed that free men regardless of color were welcome. Jews, too, were active. Had it not been for the support of men like financier Solomon Haim, the Revolution would have died of economic attrition as withering as any battle or hardship at Valley Forge.

The Battle of Bunker's Hill, *painted by John Trumbull.*
Less than two months after the confrontation at Lexington and Concord, this battle took place in which 1,054 Americans were killed or wounded. Courtesy of The Yale University Art Gallery.

Nor should one overlook the contribution of American women. Never again would there be a conflict that so enlisted the energies of the entire populace — men, women and children. Wives followed husbands into battle. Much more than camp followers, they proved to be smoke eaters involved in the thick of battle. One is reminded of the leather-tough women of Schoharie County when one reads this eyewitness account of tobacco-smoking, plug-chewing, oath-swearing soldier Mrs. Ludwig Hayes:

A woman whose husband belonged to the artillery and who was then attached to a piece in the engagement, attended with her husband at the piece the whole time. While in the act of reaching a cartridge and having one of her feet as far before the other as she could step, a cannon shot from the enemy passed directly between her legs without doing any other damage than carrying away all the lower part of her petticoat. Looking at it with apparent unconcern, she observed that it was lucky it did not pass a little higher, for in that case it might have carried away something else, and continued her occupation.

Molly Pitcher at the Battle of Monmouth, *painted by D. N. Carter. Molly Pitcher was the popular name for Mrs. Ludwig Hayes. Courtesy of The Historic Fraunces Tavern Museum.*

The Line of Battle

In the first critical days of war, the American army hung vulnerable and chaotic about Boston, discharging salvos of curses, cannonading with empty threats. There was no overall command, no definite enlistments, and no discipline save that natural to a common undertaking. Attempts had been made to bring order by appointing officers and enlisting volunteers for the rest of the year. The result was less than satisfactory. Liberty proved a heady brew; the American army was drunk on freedom and fiercely independent. When Washington took charge, he lamented that the men "regarded an officer no more than a broomstick." Indeed, when Washington galloped in to assume command, a Yankee sentry yawned and scratched in his journal that nothing much was happening.

While generations of boot-blacking British redcoats might hold with Tennyson's "Theirs not to reason why, / Theirs but to do and die," the rebels of the American army thought differently. The memoirs of a New Jersey private explain:

[The men were] sworn to be true and faithful soldiers of the Right Honorable Congress. After this we chose our officers....When on parade, our 1st lieut. came and

told us he would be glad if we would excuse him from going, which we refused; but on consideration we concluded it was better to consent; after which he said he would go; but we said, "You shall not command us, for he whose mind can change in an hour is not fit to command in the field where liberty is contended for." In the evening we chose a private in his place.

Happily, these stubborn, republican instincts were checked in the field. Thanks to the initiative of Washington and Friedrich Wilhelm Ludolf Gerhard Augustin von Steuben, a bogus German general imported under the auspices of Benjamin Franklin, American rebels learned the art of war.

The popular myth that Americans skipped from rock to boulder firing at columns of redcoats with a death wish is a myth indeed. With the exception of the retreat from Concord and Lexington and the skirmish at King's Mountain, Washington and the Continental Line strove manfully to meet the enemy on his own terms.

This meant that the infantry was drawn up in "the line of battle," opposing forces poised like so many chessmen on opposite sides of the board. There were two ranks of men, shoulder to shoulder, with a line of file-closers in the rear to take the place of fallen comrades. Occasionally, an officer would modify this formation slightly to allow for the whimsy and wrongheadedness of his command. At the battle of Guilford Court House, for instance, American general Nathanael Greene found it necessary to deploy his militia in front of a knot of picked troops instructed to blast the first man who ran away.

Baron Friedrich von Steuben Courtesy of The Independence National Park Collection.

Baron Von Steuben Drilling Troops at Valley Forge, *painted by Edwin Austin Abbey.* Courtesy of The Pennsylvania Historical and Museum Commission.

Revolutionary muskets. Top, a British "brown Bess" musket. Center, a rare 1776 musket which was a product of the Fredericksburg Armory in Virginia. Bottom, a French musket dated 1763, referred to as the "Lafayette" model because thousands were given to American troops as a result of the alliance with France. Courtesy of The Valley Forge Historical Society.

Steuben taught that the line of battle was a practical formation. The usual practice was to march within thirty yards of the enemy, drums and pipes a-playing, fire and charge with fixed bayonets. The defensive posture of one's opponent was the same line of battle, prepared to empty multiple volleys into charging troops.

Firing from the line of battle was a precise and disciplined business. According to military etiquette, all loading and shooting was done on command. Nobody bothered to aim. The volley was delivered directly in front or to the right or left as commanded. The intent was to lay down a field of fire, to create, in effect, a human shotgun.

Rapidity of fire was prized over accuracy. *The Military Medley*, a popular treatise done on soldiering in 1768, required "No recruit to be dismissed from the drill, till he is so expert with his firelock, as to load and fire fifteen times in three minutes and three-quarters." An experienced regiment would

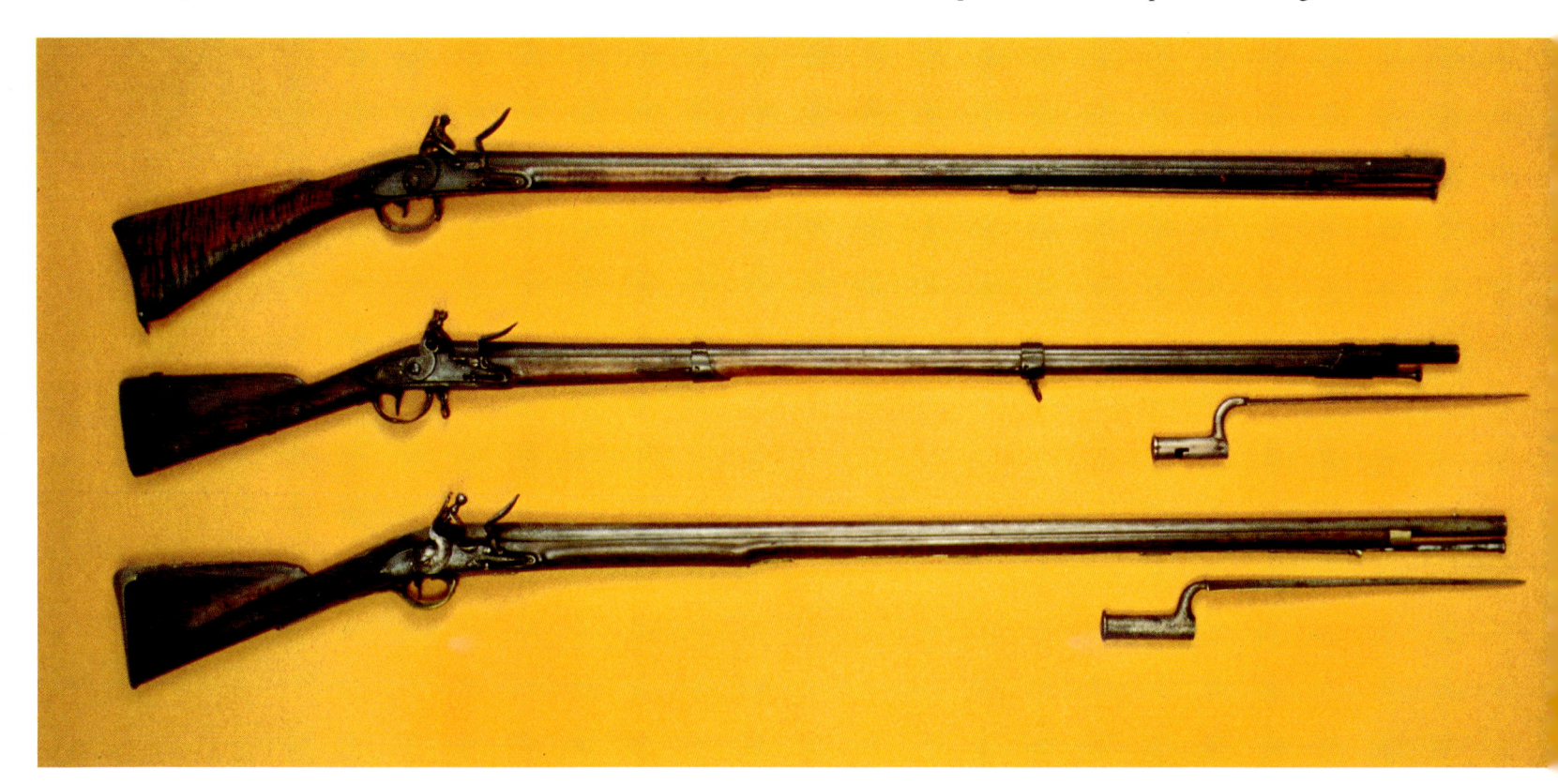

General Washington on a White Charger (*right*), *painted by an unknown artist. Courtesy of The National Gallery of Art, Washington, D.C.* Drum (*below*) *carried into battle by John Robbins at Bunker's Hill. The Latin motto inscribed on it means "Victory or Death." Courtesy of The Bostonian Society.*

American uniforms during the Revolution. From left to right: Light Infantry, First City Troop of Philadelphia (on horseback), Washington's Bodyguard, Pennsylvania Line Infantry Private, Continental Artillery Private, Massachusetts Line Infantry Lieutenant, New York Line Infantry Private, Artillery Captain, South Carolina Infantry Lieutenant, General Washington and Moylan's Dragoons. Courtesy of The Massachusetts Historical Society.

fire once every fifteen seconds — 1,000 shots in two volleys every twenty or twenty-five seconds. It was a brutal way to fight. Nothing quite so macabre would be devised till the advent of the antipersonnel bomb. A soldier, weighed down with some hundred pounds of pack and arms, stared across 30 yards of no-man's-land into the hollow eyes of brown Bess muskets on the other side. He knew, too, that those baleful eyes winking in dreadful unison were charged deep with .80 caliber bullets, buckshot and rusty nails.

He looked death in the eye and ran after it. Life was cheap in the eighteenth century. Still, the officer who threw his men into that storm of lead, raining like hailstones beating down a wheat field, could not waste human lives easily. He had desperate need of the reassurance of a hundred years of martial custom and military etiquette of which his buttons, badges, lace and brightwork were the visible presence. And yet, even these were sometimes insufficient. At the battle for Long Island, Private Joseph Martin observed "a lieutenant who appeared to have feelings not very enviable...for he ran round among the men of his company, sniveling and blubbering, praying each one if he had aught against him, declaring at the same time that he, from his heart, forgave them if they had offended him, and I gave him full credit for his assertion; for had he been at the gallows with a halter about his neck, he could not have shown more fear or penitence." And during the seven terrible years of war, there were many like him, unmanned by the carnage exacted for some unnamed, forgotten and Godforsaken hundred yards of dirt.

Nor was the terror over once a man had negotiated those hundred yards. Then troops fell to hand-to-hand fighting, each formless face assuming suddenly a fearsome clarity. Many a man died, his hands up in supplication, while a bayonet spooned out his belly.

The bayonet, the bayonet — a generation removed from the Stone Age, this was the weapon of the Revolution. The British took Bunker's Hill by bayonet. Samuel Webster cried out, "'Tis barbarous to let men be obliged to oppose Bayonets with only gun Barrells...."

When the British closed with bayonets, the result was disaster. Colonel George Hander of His Majesty's army recalled:

When Morgan's riflemen came down to Pennsylvania from Canada, flushed with success gained over Burgoyne's army, they marched to attack our light infantry under Colonel Abercrombie. The moment they appeared before him he ordered his troops to charge them with the bayonet; not one man out of four, had time to fire, and those that did had no time given them to load again: the light infantry not only dispersed them instantly but drove them for miles over the country.

In the midst of this Stone Age barbarity, Washington retaliated by arming Morgan's riflemen with spears! Indeed, medieval tools of war were almost commonplace. Pikes and spears and spontoons were especially used. One Captain Anderson, racing a rival to a British artillery piece, employed his spontoon to particular advantage, as witnessed by his commander, "Light Horse Harry" Lee:

Captain Anderson, hearing the order, also pushed for the same object and both being emulous for the prize kept pace until near the first piece, when Anderson, by putting the end of his spontoon forward into the ground, made a long leap which brought him upon the gun and gave him the honor of the prize.

Such weapons served sometimes as a badge of rank, sometimes in lieu of firearms when there were none to be had. When in 1777 Washington petitioned the Massachusetts Committee of Safety for more muskets, the Committee was obliged to reply, "Firearms cannot be procured from us that can be depended upon." They went on to say that they were practically out of undependable ones as well.

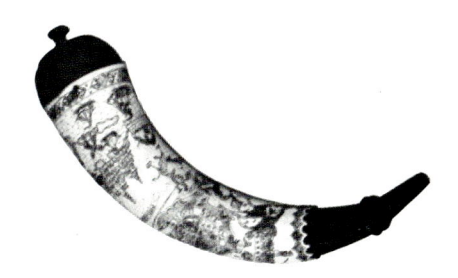

Powder horn (above), made in revolutionary times, which depicts the city of Philadelphia. Courtesy of The Valley Forge Historical Society. Broadside (below), issued in 1775 in Cambridge, Massachusetts, which calls for supplies for the new Continental army. Courtesy of The Library of Congress.

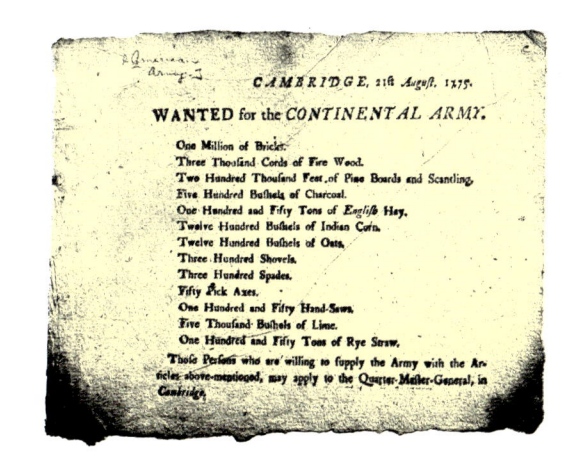

The Hardship Army

Washington's headquarters' correspondence during this time of trial had a certain wolf-at-the-door desperation. He had nothing. It seemed that every new day brought the termination of more enlistments. Troops clamored to be paid. A private in the Continental army earned less than $7.00 a month, out of which an allotment for clothing was deducted. Scant as were his wages, it was a rare thing when the trooper saw money at all, and then he would have to hide it from his fellows. When he was paid, it was often in Continental paper of dubious value. Men grew desperate for gold.

While a prisoner of the patriot army, Baroness von Riedesel, wife of one of the German mercenary commanders, observed:

[The Americans] very much prized coined money, which for them was very scarce. One of our officers' boots were completely torn. He saw that an American general

Washington Reviewing His Ragged Army at Valley Forge, *painted by William Brooks Thomas Trego. Courtesy of The Valley Forge Historical Society.*

was wearing a good pair and jestingly said to him, "I would gladly give you a guinea for them." The general immediately jumped off his horse, took the guinea, gave the officer his boots, and wearing the officer's torn pair, mounted his horse again.

Along with the scarcity of money, Washington had to contend with festering graft. One headquarters' directive specified:

It has been intimated to the general, that some officers under pretence of giving furloughs to men recovering from sickness, send them to work upon their farms for their own private emolument, at the same time, that the public is taxed with their pay....

Washington found such accusations hard to believe, but he promised to punish the guilty, nevertheless. However, even with dire warnings hanging over the soldiers' heads, corruption still flourished. No wonder men's thoughts turned to their own farms as they traipsed through fertile American valleys despoiled by the British.

Private Joseph Martin recalled:

Early next morning we marched again and came up with the rear of the British army.... We had ample opportunity to see the devastation they made in their rout; cattle killed and lying about the fields and pastures, some just in the position they were in when shot down, others with a small spot of skin taken off their hind quarters and a mess of steak taken out; household furniture hacked and broken to pieces; wells filled up and mechanics' and farmers' tools destroyed. It was in the height of the season of cherries; the innocent industrious creatures could not climb the trees for the fruit, but universally cut them down.

To wash his white breeches, powder his hair and clean brightwork, the British soldier labored three hours a day, day in and day out. It was a regimen strange to the American forces, who at Valley Forge and Morristown in 1780 pitched what tents they had "without shoes and stockings, and working half leg deep in snow."

Falling back from New Jersey across the Delaware, General Washington watched the retreat of 6,000 men "entirely naked and most so thinly clad as to be unfit for service." The prospect was demoralizing. The crisis could hardly be overstated. Hunger and hardship had so ravaged his troops that Washington confided privately that unless he had more men "the game will be pretty well up."

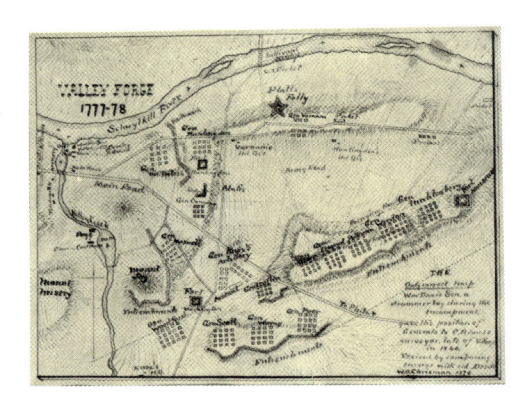

This map of Valley Forge shows the positions of the generals during the winter of 1777-78. Although the map was not made until 1840, its information was verified by William Davis, who had been a drummer boy during the encampment. Courtesy of The Valley Forge Historical Society.

A medical chest used at Valley Forge. Courtesy of The Valley Forge Historical Society.

Even the British, dogging his heels, were bewildered by the evident collapse of the army from want of supplies. Surveying a litter of dead rebels left in the wake of an American retreat, one officer remarked, "Many of the Rebels who were killed…were without shoes or stockings, & several were observed to have only linen drawers…without any proper shirt or waistcoat…also in great want of blankets…they must suffer extremely."

At Valley Forge, surgeon Albigence Waldo, who had signed on with the 1st Connecticut, watched the pitiless attrition of his friends and comrades. During the day, he struggled to maintain military decorum and put a bluff, soldierly face on everything. At night, he poured his anguish into his letters. "There comes a soldier," he wrote, "his bare feet are seen through his worn-out shoes, his legs nearly naked from the tattered remains of an only pair of stockings, his breeches are not sufficient to cover his nakedness…his whole appearance pictures a person forsaken & discouraged. He…cries…I am sick, my feet lame, my legs sore, my body covered with this tormenting itch."

The Healing Trade

To have been Albigence Waldo must have been a terrible thing. Here was a man sworn to heal, to minister, to make well. Yet, virtually his only remedy was a kind word. His scant and errant eighteenth-century knowledge of medicine fell far short of the critical need.

For the eighteenth century is aptly styled the romantic period of American medicine, marked by imagination rather than reason. In a world where one's own mortality was painfully apparent, most people lived closer to death than to a doctor. For some it was a good thing, too. The underschooled and ill-equipped men who called themselves "physician" practiced a rugged brand of medicine.

The best of the colonial doctors knew how to set a broken limb and how to remove a bullet. Their doctor's bag contained homemade bandages, a few drugs, syringes, hot-water bottles of pewter and crockery, knives, saws, and a mortar and pestle for mixing prescriptions according to exacting requirements like "a pretty draught" and "enough to lie on a jackknife's point."

Among a people who ardently believed in the doctrine of natural rights, there was considerable sentiment that the practice of medicine was an inherent right. One might as well be a doctor as anything else. Indeed, a resident of Huntington, Long Island, during this period recalled being interrupted at his tavern dinner by "a band of the town politicians in short jackets and trowsers. Among the rest," he said, "was a fellow with a worsted cap and great black fists. They stiled him doctor…he had been a shoemaker in town and was a notable fellow at his trade, but happening two years ago to cure an old woman of a pestilent mortal disease, he thereby acquired the character of a physician, was applied to from all quarters, and finding the practise of physick a more profitable business than cobling, he laid aside his awls and leather, got himself some gallipots, and instead of cobling of soles, fell to cobling of human bodies."

Moreover, the healing trade offered opportunity for individual expression, something much appreciated by nascent Americans. Among the various nostrums and panaceas available to the doctor were a whole army of depleting remedies: purges, vomits, sweats, blisters, bloodletting, and poultices of garlic, onions, radishes, freshly chewed tobacco and gunpowder.

One might hold with the doctor who favored dispensing antimony, "that very active metal, and which, mild as it was, left…patients very commonly with a pretty strong conviction that they had taken *something* that did not exactly agree with them." Or, one might follow the pioneering practice of John Saffin who advocated this remedy: "Take an egg and boil it very hard, then pull off the shell, and put it as hot as you can well endure, into the fundament of the patient grieved and when it is much abated of heat, put another egg in the same manner and it will cure."

America looked like a gold mine to any ambitious peddler of pills and panaceas. Poor nutrition, ill-constructed and crowded houses, elementary notions of sanitation, a life of exposure and toil left the colonists open to a host of afflictions. Epidemics of malaria, cholera, typhoid, scurvy, scarlet fever, yellow fever, diphtheria, smallpox, tuberculosis and influenza infected the countryside from Georgia to Maine.

Malaria was widespread and so endemic in America that it came to be perceived as a national trait. The disease gave Americans that gaunt look which now survives chiefly in the cartoonist's characterization of lean-visaged Uncle Sam.

And war brought a more terrible enemy than the British. The mysterious and evil "bloody flux," which today we know as dysentery, stole silently

Surgical instruments used by military doctors during the Revolution. Courtesy of The Armed Forces Institute of Pathology.

throughout the country. Abigail Adams wept in Braintree, Massachusetts, "The desolation of war is not so distressing as the havoc made by this pestilence. Some poor parents are mourning the loss of three, four, and five children; and some families are wholly stripped of every member....'Tis a dreadful time with the whole province. Sickness and death are in almost every family."

The colonial army lost many soldiers to dysentery. In 1775, both American forces bivouacked in Cambridge, and British forces in Boston suffered. Throughout the war, the disease so tormented the contesting armies that it was familiarly called "camp distemper" by the troops. The following scene typifies the distrust many soldiers had in doctors and medicines — but even more — it shows how well-founded their feelings were.

"Hey, mate, are you one of those new Connecticut lads they attached to our company?"

"Yup."

"Ha! Well, we don't want any wooden nutmegs around here."

"A remark, sir, that could send you picking up your teeth with a rake."

"Now, now, Nutmeg, no offense meant. Where's the rest of your Connecticut boys?"

"Those that left Fort Mifflin alive are mostly down with camp distemper."

"Why, there's hardly a one of us that's not fighting the flux or pneumonia, as well as the British. Lord, boy, don't you know the old man told me that half our boys serving under Montgomery and Benedict Arnold at Quebec came down with smallpox! Then there was plenty that didn't survive the variolation — introducing that fetid pox pus into a man's arm — goes against God's laws if you ask me."

"Would you rather have the pox?"

"Course not, course not. It's just that I don't trust those bonecutters and herb doctors. Heck, I was in that so-called hospital once. Doc came after me with the latest scientific curiosity called a 'scarificator.' Know what kind of a toy that is? This scarificator is a little box instrument for bleeding — makes several cuts at once. 'Bleed until you faint!' the man says, and takes twenty to forty ounces of blood. Lord, that's doctors for you; they up and invent something that'll kill you seven times faster than nature. The Almighty God done already invented leeches — what use have we of *scarificators.*"

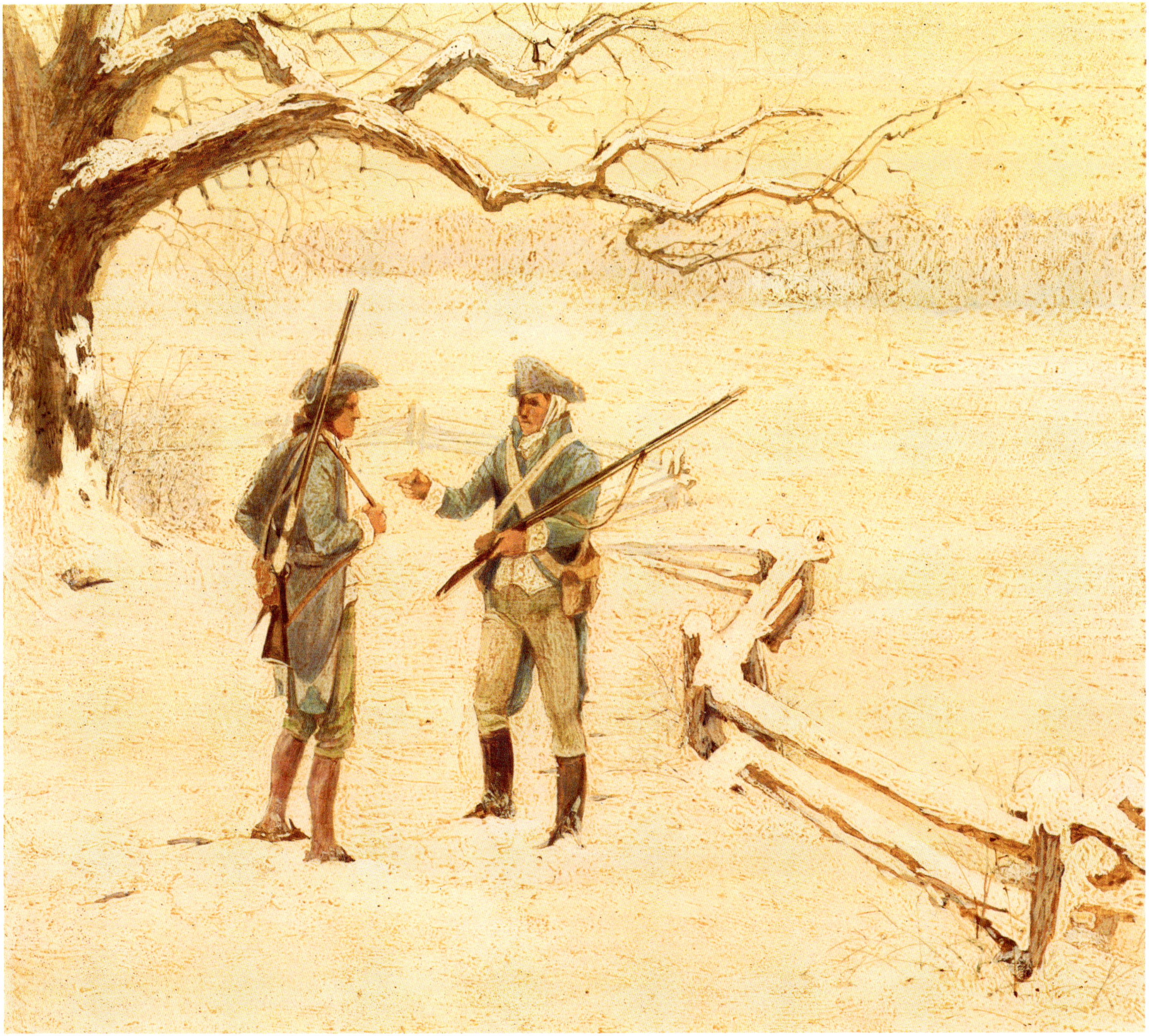

*Lieutenant General Charles Cornwallis
Courtesy of The Virginia State Library.*

Detail of an engraving showing General John Burgoyne's captured army at a prison camp in Charlottesville, Virginia. Suspecting that the British would send these troops back into battle if they were released, Congress refused them parole. Courtesy of The Library of Congress.

"But these are learned men!"

"Learned men pshaw! Take our surgeon general for instance — not a brain in his head. He says that the Continental soldier exposed to wet and cold — that's you and me, boy — can ward off fevers by pouring a half pint of rum into each boot. I'd rather be in the Lord's company tomorrow than trust my mortal parts to the hands of a doctor."

"You ought to be grateful."

"The only thing this soldier is grateful for is a little lady in Princeton who made the war seem easier one night. Now look, Nutmeg, if you're going to join up with our company, you gotta stand sentry like everybody else. Go relieve Laommi Wolcott. You'll find him easy enough. Just follow the blood in the snow — he ain't got no boots either."

The Dawn of a Nation

It is hard to believe that such men as these eeked out a momentous victory, although so ill equipped they were reduced to scavenging for cannonballs — snatching a still-rolling British ball to fire back at the enemy, so destitute that they ate their boots in the North and swallowed dried alligator in the South. It is strange that this patch-and-gristle rebel army had defeated the largest and best-equipped expeditionary force ever mustered by the eighteenth century's most powerful nation.

Seven years before, no one would have guessed the outcome. Futurity was decidedly unfathomable.

The war waged so long in the North came to an end in the South. Private Joseph Martin was there at the siege of Yorktown:

The whole number, American and French, was ninety-two cannon, mortars, and howitzers. Our flagstaff was in the ten-gun battery, upon the right of the whole. I was in the trenches the day that the batteries were to be opened. All were upon the tiptoe of expectation and impatience to see the signal given to open the whole line of batteries, which was to be the hoisting of the American flag in the ten-gun battery. About noon the much-wished-for signal went up. I confess I felt a secret pride swell my heart when I saw the "star-spangled banner" waving majestically in the very faces of our implacable adversaries. It appeared like an omen of success to our enterprise, and so it proved in reality.

Surrender of Lord Cornwallis at Yorktown, *painted by John Trumbull. Actually, it was General Charles O'Hara (standing center) who surrendered to General Benjamin Lincoln (to his left on horseback). Lord Cornwallis, absent due to illness, had deputized O'Hara to surrender in his place. General Washington (in background at right) refused to accept surrender from a deputy and appointed Lincoln to act in his behalf. Courtesy of The Yale University Art Gallery.*

On October 19, 1781, the British filed out of Yorktown and laid down their arms. The British band, not without irony, played a nursery tune, "The World Turned Upside Down." Although the Continental army would keep the field for an additional two years, Yorktown marked the real end of the war of arms. Sometime later, on a brisk September morning in 1783, the war was ended in good earnest. The Treaty of Paris, ending hostilities and establishing independence, was signed with a flourish.

A revolution that had stirred in the minds of men, that had been advocated and disputed in tavern and taproom, pulpit and pew; a revolution bought dearly on the battlefield had at last come to pass. We the people were endowed with a national identity — and a new responsibility. After the signing, a bystander referred to the struggle as the "War of Independence." Dr. Franklin turned on him. "Say rather the War of Revolution," he said. "The War of Independence is yet to be fought."

Washington's Farewell to His Officers, *painted by Alonzo Chappel. Courtesy of The Chicago Historical Society.*

Revolutionary cannons stand silently at Valley Forge.

COLONIAL GLOSSARY

A SPONGING: An act of drinking.
ANT-BEAR: An anteater.
BETTY LAMP: A lamp consisting of a shallow, lidded, metal vessel with a small spout for a coarse wick fueled by tallow, grease or oil. This lamp was usually hung by a hook and chain.
BLACKJACK TANKARD: A vessel for beer or ale, usually of wax-coated leather.
BOSTON PORT BILL: An act passed by Parliament to close the port of Boston after the Boston Tea Party, thereby ruining the port's trade; one of the infamous Coercive Acts.
COERCIVE ACTS: A group of acts passed by Parliament after the Boston Tea Party for the closing of the port of Boston until the British East India Company was reimbursed for the tea that was destroyed.
DUROY: A coarse, woolen cloth made in England in the eighteenth century which was used chiefly for men's wear.
FIRKIN: A small wooden vessel of indeterminate size; usually one-quarter barrel.
FIVEBLED: To increase fivefold.
FLIP: A drink, popular in eighteenth-century England and colonial America, consisting of sweetened rum and beer or ale which is heated often with a hot poker or loggerhead.
FOOTPAD: A person who robs pedestrians; a highwayman.
FOURBLED: To increase fourfold.
FROWSTING: To lounge.
GALLIPOT: A small, usually ceramic vessel with a small mouth used by apothecaries to hold medicines.
GALLOWAY PLAN: A moderate plan of colonial union with Britain which failed to pass.
THE GREAT HORN SPOON: A phrase commonly used as an epithet as in "by the great horn spoon."
GROANING BOARD: A table.

HOTCHPOT: A thick soup of meat and vegetables.
HUCKABACK: A strong fabric made of linen or cotton and linen which has an uneven surface produced by alternately crossing the filling threads. This fabric is often used for towels.
JERSEY LIGHTNING: A variety of liquor made from frozen, fermented apple cider.
KILDERKIN: A cask which is about half the size of a common barrel.
LAUDANUM: Any of various opium preparations.
PERRY QUINCE: An alcoholic drink made from fermented pear juice.
PUMPKIN SUPPAWN: A hasty pudding made of oatmeal boiled in water.
QUEBEC BILL: A bill that proclaimed recognition of the Catholic Church in Quebec.
ROLLICHES: A type of sausage made in a bag of tripe and then sliced and fried.
SOUSE: A type of food such as pigs' feet or fish which is pickled.
SPONTOON: A half-pike formerly borne by subordinate officers of infantry.
STONEWALL: A strong alcoholic drink made from hard cider and rum.
SUFFOLK RESOLVES: A group of resolutions passed in Suffolk, Massachusetts, and adopted by Congress in Philadelphia which (1) declared the Coercive Acts unconstitutional, (2) urged the people to form their own government, collect taxes and withhold them from the British until the Coercive Acts were repealed, (3) advised the people to arm and form their own militia and (4) recommended economic sanctions against Britain.
TOSS POT: A large cup.
TUNNEKIN: A large barrel.

The unanimous Declaration

When in the Course of human events it becomes n[ecessary]
a[ss]ume among the powers of the earth, the separate and equal station to which the Laws of Natur[e]
should declare the causes which impel them to the separation. —————— We hol[d]
with certain unalienable Rights, that among these are Life, Liberty and the pursuit of H[appiness]
powers from the consent of the governed. — That whenever any Form of Government becomes
Government, laying its foundation on such principles and organizing its powers in such [form]
will dictate that Governments long established should not be changed for light and transient
evils are sufferable, than to right themselves by abolishing the forms to which they are accus[tomed]
vinces a design to reduce them under absolute Despotism, it is their right, it is their duty to
been the patient sufferance of these Colonies; and such is now the necessity which constrains th[em]
Britain is a history of repeated injuries and usurpations, all having in direct object the establi[shment]
world. —————— He has refused his Assent to Laws, the most wholesome and nece[ssary]
and pressing importance, unless suspended in their operation till his Assent should be obta[ined]
pass other Laws for the accommodation of large districts of people, unless those people would reli[nquish]
to tyrants only. —————— He has called together legislative bodies at places unusual, uncomfo[rtable]
compliance with his measures. —————— He has dissolved Representative Houses repeatedly, fo[r]
a long time, after such dissolutions, to cause others to be elected; whereby the Legislative powers
ing in the mean time exposed to all the dangers of invasion from without, and convulsions wi[thin]
ting the Laws for Naturalization of Foreigners; refusing to pass others to encourage their migration
Administration of Justice, by refusing his Assent to Laws for establishing Judiciary powers